McGraw-Hill E

500 Auditing and Attestation Questions

FOR THE

CPA Exam

Also in the McGraw-Hill Education 500 Questions Series:

McGraw-Hill Education

500 Auditing and Attestation Questions

FOR THE

CPA Exam

Denise M. Stefano, CPA, CGMA, MBA, and
Darrel Surett, CPA

New York Chicago San Francisco Athens London Madrid
Mexico City Milan New Delhi Singapore Sydney Toronto

1 2 3 4 5 6 7 8 9 10   QFR/QFR   1 0 9 8 7 6 5 4

ISBN   978-0-07-180709-8
MHID   0-07-180709-8

e-ISBN   978-0-07-180710-4
e-MHID   0-07-180710-1

Library of Congress Control Number 2014934327

McGraw-Hill Education products are available at special quantity discounts to use as premiums and sales promotions or for use in corporate training programs. To contact a representative, please visit the Contact Us pages at www.mhprofessional.com.

This book is printed on acid-free paper.

CONTENTS

INTRODUCTION

Congratulations! You've taken a big step toward CPA Exam success by purchasing *McGraw-Hill Education: 500 Auditing and Attestation Questions for the CPA Exam*. This book gives you 500 multiple-choice questions that cover all the most essential material for the Auditing and Attestation section of the CPA Exam. Each question is clearly explained in the answer key. The questions will give you valuable independent practice to supplement your other studies.

You might be the kind of student who needs extra study a few weeks before the exam for a final review. Or you might be the kind of student who puts off preparing until the last minute before the exam. No matter what your preparation style, you will benefit from reviewing these 500 questions, which closely parallel the content, format, and degree of difficulty of the questions on the actual CPA Exam. These questions and the explanations in the answer key are the ideal last-minute study tools for those final weeks before the test.

If you practice with all the questions and answers in this book, we are certain you will build the skills and confidence needed to excel on the CPA Exam. Good luck!

—Editors of McGraw-Hill Education

CHAPTER 1

Proper Use of the Term *Audit* and an Overview of Auditing

1. Which of the following standards-setting bodies has authority to issue auditing standards for financial statement audits of nonissuers?
   I. Auditing Standards Board
   II. Public Company Accounting Oversight Board

   (A) I only
   (B) II only
   (C) Both I and II
   (D) Neither I nor II

2. Whenever an independent expert is brought in to examine financial statements with hopes of adding credibility, that engagement and reporting process is known as an:
   I. Audit
   II. Attestation

   (A) I only
   (B) II only
   (C) Both I and II
   (D) Neither I nor II

3. A CPA performed the following engagements in February of Year 3. Which is considered an attestation engagement?
   I. Audit of Year 2 financial statements
   II. Examination of Year 4's proposed financial information

   (A) I only
   (B) II only
   (C) Both I and II
   (D) Neither I nor II

4. After an audit, the financial statements are the responsibility of:
   I. The independent auditor
   II. The management of the reporting company

   (A) I only
   (B) II only
   (C) Both I and II
   (D) Neither I nor II

5. According to the generally accepted auditing reporting standards, which of the following must be expressed in a standard auditor's report?
   I. The auditor's conclusion that consistent accounting principles were applied from period to period
   II. The auditor's opinion that the financial statement disclosures and footnotes are sufficient and appropriate in the circumstances

   (A) I only
   (B) II only
   (C) Both I and II
   (D) Neither I nor II

6. Lara is a covered member in an audit engagement. Which of the following cannot work in any capacity for a company being audited by Lara?
   I. Lara's spouse
   II. Lara's dependent daughter

   (A) I only
   (B) II only
   (C) Both I and II
   (D) Neither I nor II

7. Which of the following is correct regarding a covered member of an audit engagement?
   I. If the dependent child of a covered member owns $300 worth of stock in an audit client, the covered member would still be independent if the dependent child were under age five.
   II. If the spouse of a covered member owns an immaterial indirect financial interest in the audit client, the covered member would still be independent.

   (A) I only
   (B) II only
   (C) Both I and II
   (D) Neither I nor II

8. In which of the following situations regarding independence would the concept of materiality NOT apply?
   I. Auditing firm owns one share of stock in a publicly traded company under audit. The share is held in a brokerage account.
   II. Auditor's spouse owns one share in a mutual fund that owns shares in a client company. The client is a publicly traded company.
   (A) I only
   (B) II only
   (C) Both I and II
   (D) Neither I nor II

9. A violation of the profession's independence standards most likely would have occurred when:
   I. The daughter of a covered member is employed as a parking lot attendant and makes cash tips at the client under audit
   II. The CPA issued an unmodified opinion on the Year 2 financial statements when fees for the Year 1 audit were unpaid
   (A) I only
   (B) II only
   (C) Both I and II
   (D) Neither I nor II

10. In an audit of financial statements of a nonissuer in accordance with generally accepted auditing standards, an auditor is required to:
    I. Perform tests of controls to evaluate the effectiveness of the entity's accounting system
    II. Document the auditor's understanding of the entity's internal control structure
    (A) I only
    (B) II only
    (C) Both I and II
    (D) Neither I nor II

11. For which of the following attestation engagements does a CPA gather evidence and then provide an opinion regarding fair presentation of financial information?
    I. Examination of forward-looking financial information
    II. Audits of historic financial statements
    (A) I only
    (B) II only
    (C) Both I and II
    (D) Neither I nor II

CHAPTER 2

Audit Planning and Risk Assessment

12. Which of the following should be considered by a CPA prior to acceptance of an audit engagement of a nonissuer?
    - I. The quality of the accounting records
    - II. The future plans for the company

    (A) I only
    (B) II only
    (C) Both I and II
    (D) Neither I nor II

13. Inquiries of the predecessor auditor prior to acceptance of the engagement should include specific questions regarding:
    - I. Disagreements with management as to accounting principles and auditing procedures
    - II. The integrity of management

    (A) I only
    (B) II only
    (C) Both I and II
    (D) Neither I nor II

14. A CPA should decide NOT to accept a new client for an audit engagement if:
    - I. The CPA lacks an understanding of the client's industry and accounting principles prior to acceptance
    - II. The client's management has unusually high turnover

    (A) I only
    (B) II only
    (C) Both I and II
    (D) Neither I nor II

15. Which of the following procedures would an auditor likely perform in the planning stage of a financial statement audit?

    I. Obtaining a signed engagement letter from the client's management
    II. Examining documents to detect violations of laws and regulations having a material effect on the financial statements

    (A) I only
    (B) II only
    (C) Both I and II
    (D) Neither I nor II

16. Which of the following procedures is likely to be performed in the planning stage of the audit?

    I. Determining the extent of involvement of specialists and internal auditors
    II. External confirmation of client accounts receivables

    (A) I only
    (B) II only
    (C) Both I and II
    (D) Neither I nor II

17. All of the following are correct regarding an auditor's understanding with a potential client prior to beginning an audit **except**:

    (A) The understanding should cover the responsibilities of the independent auditor.
    (B) The understanding should cover the limitations of the engagement.
    (C) The understanding should be in the form of an engagement letter in order to be in conformity with auditing standards.
    (D) The understanding should list the audit fees and frequency of billing.

18. Management's responsibilities in the engagement letter include which of the following?

    I. Adjusting the financial statements to correct material misstatements
    II. Identifying and ensuring that the entity complies with laws and regulations
    III. Selecting and applying accounting policies

    (A) I and II only
    (B) II and III only
    (C) I and III only
    (D) I, II, and III

19. Which of the following is correct regarding the auditor's preliminary judgment about materiality?
    I. The auditor utilizes the results of the internal control questionnaire.
    II. The auditor utilizes annualized interim financial statements.
    (A) I only
    (B) II only
    (C) Both I and II
    (D) Neither I nor II

20. Which of the following procedures would an auditor likely perform in planning a financial statement audit?
    I. Selecting a sample of vendors' invoices for comparison to receiving reports
    II. Coordinating the assistance of entity personnel in data preparation
    III. Reading the current year's interim financial statements
    (A) II only
    (B) II and III only
    (C) I, II, and III
    (D) III only

21. Which of the following will cause the auditor to assess inherent risk as high?
    I. Complex transactions with third parties are discovered.
    II. No related-party transactions are discovered.
    III. Management relies heavily on estimates in the financial statements.
    (A) I and II only
    (B) I, II, and III
    (C) I and III only
    (D) III only

22. Inherent risk:
    I. Would not be present if the company were not being audited
    II. Is assessed by the auditor, but this assessment has no bearing on the actual amount of inherent risk present
    (A) I only
    (B) II only
    (C) Both I and II
    (D) Neither I nor II

23. Which of the following risks is assessed by the auditor in the planning stage?
    I. Inherent risk
    II. Control risk

    (A) I only
    (B) II only
    (C) Both I and II
    (D) Neither I nor II

24. Which of the following risks is assessed by the auditor but the auditor's assessment has no bearing on the actual amount of risk present?
    I. Control risk
    II. Inherent risk

    (A) I only
    (B) II only
    (C) Both I and II
    (D) Neither I nor II

25. Which of the following is a component of audit risk?
    I. Detection risk
    II. Inherent risk

    (A) I only
    (B) II only
    (C) Both I and II
    (D) Neither I nor II

26. An auditor can lower overall audit risk by reducing:

    (A) Inherent risk
    (B) Control risk
    (C) Detection risk
    (D) All of the above

27. In an audit under GAAS, when an auditor increases the assessed level of control risk because certain control activities were determined to be ineffective, the auditor most likely would:

    (A) Lower detection risk
    (B) Decrease the extent of tests of details
    (C) Increase inherent risk
    (D) Perform tests of controls

28. Which of the following is correct?
    I. Control risk is not part of overall audit risk, although it is assessed by the auditor.
    II. Detection risk is part of overall audit risk, but it is not assessed by the auditor.
    (A) I only
    (B) II only
    (C) Both I and II
    (D) Neither I nor II

29. Inherent risk is:
    I. Not influenced by the amount of work or other testing performed by the independent auditor
    II. A characteristic of the accounting system and the personnel who work in that system
    (A) I only
    (B) II only
    (C) Both I and II
    (D) Neither I nor II

30. Control risk is:
    I. Influenced by the amount of work or other testing performed by the independent auditor
    II. Mitigated by good internal controls
    (A) I only
    (B) II only
    (C) Both I and II
    (D) Neither I nor II

31. If an auditor assesses both the inherent risk and the control risk for a particular account to be high:
    I. The auditor must then set the acceptable level of detection risk for that account to a relatively low level
    II. The auditor will perform more substantive testing in that area
    (A) I only
    (B) II only
    (C) Both I and II
    (D) Neither I nor II

32. By gathering more evidence through substantive testing, an auditor can reduce:
    I. Detection risk
    II. Control risk
    III. Inherent risk

    (A) I and III only
    (B) I and II only
    (C) I only
    (D) I, II, and III

33. With regard to overall audit risk, an auditor's decision to reduce detection risk ultimately reduces:
    I. Control risk
    II. Audit risk
    III. Inherent risk

    (A) I and II only
    (B) II and III only
    (C) I, II, and III
    (D) II only

34. An auditor wants to reduce detection risk. To achieve this goal, the auditor can:
    I. Do more substantive testing or can gather evidence of a better quality
    II. Perform more testing earlier in the audit

    (A) I only
    (B) II only
    (C) Both I and II
    (D) Neither I nor II

35. On the basis of audit evidence gathered and evaluated, an auditor decides to increase the assessed level of control risk, and therefore the risk of material misstatement, from that originally planned. To achieve an overall audit risk level that is substantially the same as the planned audit risk level, the auditor would:

    (A) Decrease detection risk
    (B) Decrease substantive testing
    (C) Increase inherent risk
    (D) Increase materiality levels

36. In a financial statement audit, inherent risk is evaluated to help an auditor assess which of the following?

   (A) The internal audit department's objectivity in reporting a material misstatement of a financial statement assertion it detects to the audit committee

   (B) The risk that the internal control system will not detect a material misstatement of a financial statement assertion

   (C) The susceptibility of the financial statements to a material misstatement, assuming there are no related controls

   (D) The risk that the audit procedures implemented will not detect a material misstatement of a financial statement assertion

37. There is an inverse relationship between detection risk and the auditor's assessment of:

   I. Inherent risk

   II. Control risk

   (A) I only

   (B) II only

   (C) Both I and II

   (D) Neither I nor II

38. Which of the following is an example of fraudulent financial reporting?

   I. An employee steals inventory and the shrinkage is recorded in cost of goods sold.

   II. Company management changes inventory count tags and overstates ending inventory while understating cost of goods sold.

   (A) I only

   (B) II only

   (C) Both I and II

   (D) Neither I nor II

39. Which of the following is an example of fraudulent financial reporting?

   I. The treasurer stealing cash from the company

   II. The recording of false sales prior to year-end to help reach company sales forecasts

   (A) I only

   (B) II only

   (C) Both I and II

   (D) Neither I nor II

40. If a company incorrectly applies an accounting principle to a significant transaction, and the misstatement was other than intentional, which of the following could describe the misstatement?
    I. Error
    II. Fraud

    (A) I only
    (B) II only
    (C) Both I and II
    (D) Neither I nor II

41. Special consideration must be given to the possibility that fraud exists during which of the following phases of the audit?
    I. Assessment of inherent risk
    II. Assessment of control risk
    III. Substantive testing

    (A) I and II only
    (B) I, II, and III
    (C) I and III only
    (D) I only

42. Which of the following is a fraud risk factor?
    I. Unauthorized client transaction
    II. Unusual client delay

    (A) I only
    (B) II only
    (C) Both I and II
    (D) Neither I nor II

43. Which of the following should be viewed by the auditor as a fraud risk factor?
    I. Company officials have issued a report stating that they expect earnings per share to double in the current year.
    II. There have been no missing documents and no delays in delivering the documents.

    (A) I only
    (B) II only
    (C) Both I and II
    (D) Neither I nor II

44. Which of the following should be viewed by the auditor as a fraud risk factor?
    I. The threat of bankruptcy
    II. The absence of significant competition
    (A) I only
    (B) II only
    (C) Both I and II
    (D) Neither I nor II

45. Which of the following analytical procedures is likely to aid the auditor in evaluating the risk of improper revenue recognition due to fraud?
    I. Comparison of sales volume to production capacity
    II. Trend analysis of revenues and sales returns by month
    (A) I only
    (B) II only
    (C) Both I and II
    (D) Neither I nor II

46. Which of the following is a component of the fraud triangle?
    I. Ability to rationalize fraud
    II. Pressure to commit fraud
    (A) I only
    (B) II only
    (C) Both I and II
    (D) Neither I nor II

47. Which of the following is a fraud risk factor regarding fraudulent financial statements?
    I. Large amounts of cash are kept on hand overnight.
    II. The company is being audited for the first time in order to issue equity securities to the public.
    III. The company recently announced that it expects earnings per share to double.
    (A) I and II only
    (B) II only
    (C) I, II, and III
    (D) II and III only

48. Which of the following is a fraud risk factor regarding an opportunity to commit fraudulent financial statements?

I. Significant, unusual, or highly complex transactions are recorded near the end of the year.

II. A number of reported balances are based on significant estimations.

(A) I only
(B) II only
(C) Both I and II
(D) Neither I nor II

49. Which of the following is viewed as a fraud risk factor that indicates that management or other employees have the incentive to carry out fraudulent financial reporting?

I. There is a high turnover of senior management.

II. There are unreasonable demands on the independent auditor, such as time restraints.

(A) I only
(B) II only
(C) Both I and II
(D) Neither I nor II

50. Which of the following is viewed as a fraud risk factor that indicates that management or other employees have the incentive or pressure to carry out fraudulent financial reporting?

I. Decline in customer demand

II. Negative cash flows from operations

III. Company plans to obtain additional debt financing

(A) I, II, and III
(B) II and III only
(C) I and II only
(D) I and III only

51. Which of the following would NOT heighten an auditor's concern about the risk of intentional manipulation of financial statements?

I. Insiders recently purchased additional shares of the entity's stock.

II. Management places substantial emphasis on meeting earnings projections.

III. Management is dominated by several top executives.

IV. Inventory is comprised mostly of small, high-dollar items.

(A) I only
(B) II and III only
(C) I, III, and IV only
(D) I and II only

52. At which stage of the audit may fraud risk factors for misappropriation of assets be identified?
    I. Planning
    II. Internal control
    III. Evidence gathering

    (A) I and II only
    (B) II and III only
    (C) I and III only
    (D) I, II, and III

53. Which of the following factors would most likely heighten an auditor's concern about the risk of fraudulent financial reporting?
    I. Large amounts of liquid assets that are easily convertible into cash
    II. Financial management's participation in the initial selection of accounting principles
    III. An overly complex organizational structure involving unusual lines of authority

    (A) III only
    (B) II and III only
    (C) I, II, and III
    (D) I and III only

54. The auditor's responsibility to detect fraud would change if the fraud was caused by:
    I. Collusion
    II. Management override of controls

    (A) I only
    (B) II only
    (C) Both I and II
    (D) Neither I nor II

55. Which of the following statements reflects an auditor's responsibility for detecting errors and fraud?

    (A) An auditor is responsible for detecting employee errors and fraud, but not for discovering fraud involving employee collusion or management override.
    (B) An auditor is not responsible for detecting errors and fraud unless the application of GAAS would result in such detection.
    (C) An auditor should design the audit to provide reasonable assurance of detecting errors and fraud that are material to the financial statements.
    (D) An auditor should plan the audit to detect errors and fraud that are caused by departures from GAAP.

56. If management or employees have high personal debts and company lay-offs are anticipated, which leg of the fraud triangle would these fraud risk factors relate to?

    (A) Incentive to commit fraudulent financial reporting
    (B) Opportunity to commit misappropriation of assets
    (C) Opportunity to commit fraudulent financial reporting
    (D) Incentive to commit misappropriation of assets

57. Which of the following should be viewed as fraud risk factors that point to incentives or pressure for employees to misappropriate assets?

     I. Compensation levels inconsistent with expectations
    II. Inadequate segregation of duties

    (A) I only
    (B) II only
    (C) Both I and II
    (D) Neither I nor II

58. An auditor would likely assess inherent risk to be high in which of the following situations?

     I. Employees are not required to take vacations.
    II. Management does not have an adequate understanding of the information technology in use by the company.

    (A) I only
    (B) II only
    (C) Both I and II
    (D) Neither I nor II

59. If a company is planning on raising additional financial capital in the near future by issuing either bonds or shares of stock, the auditor would likely consider this a fraud risk factor for intentional manipulation because the company might want to increase its:

     I. Reported net income
    II. Debt-to-equity ratio

    (A) I only
    (B) II only
    (C) Both I and II
    (D) Neither I nor II

60. If brainstorming sessions reveal no significant fraud risk factors, which of the following is NOT likely to be included in an auditor's inquiry of management while obtaining information to identify the risks of material misstatement due to fraud?
    I. Does management have knowledge of fraud or suspect fraud?
    II. Does management have programs to mitigate fraud risk?
    (A) I only
    (B) II only
    (C) Both I and II
    (D) Neither I nor II

61. In every audit, regardless of the outcome of the brainstorming sessions, there exists a presumption of fraud risk in which of the following areas?
    I. Recognition of revenue
    II. Management override of internal control
    (A) I only
    (B) II only
    (C) Both I and II
    (D) Neither I nor II

62. Overstating ending inventory:
    I. Results in an understatement of cost of goods sold
    II. Results in an overstatement of net income
    (A) I only
    (B) II only
    (C) Both I and II
    (D) Neither I nor II

63. Which of the following is required on an audit?
    I. Make a legal determination of whether fraud has occurred
    II. Test appropriateness of adjusting journal entries
    (A) I only
    (B) II only
    (C) Both I and II
    (D) Neither I nor II

64. A basic premise underlying the application of analytical procedures is that:
  I. Plausible relationships among data may reasonably be expected to exist and continue in the absence of known conditions to the contrary
  II. Analytical procedures can substitute for tests of certain balances and transactions

(A) I only
(B) II only
(C) Both I and II
(D) Neither I nor II

65. Which of the following is NOT an analytical procedure?
  I. Developing the expected current year sales based on the sales trend of the prior five years
  II. Estimating payroll expense by multiplying the number of employees by the average hourly wage rate and number of hours worked

(A) I only
(B) II only
(C) Both I and II
(D) Neither I nor II

66. In which stage of the audit would analytical procedures NOT likely be performed?
  I. Overall review stage
  II. Planning stage

(A) I only
(B) II only
(C) Both I and II
(D) Neither I nor II

67. Which of the following is correct regarding Statements on Auditing Standards?
  I. Statements on Auditing Standards mostly apply to audits of issuers but audits of nonissuers are permitted (but not required) to follow these standards also.
  II. Auditors will not be held responsible for a violation of Statements on Auditing Standards if the auditor was not aware of the standard.

(A) I only
(B) II only
(C) Both I and II
(D) Neither I nor II

CHAPTER 3

Understanding and Testing of Internal Control

68. Management's ability to foresee problems and take steps in advance to prevent problems is known as:
   I.   Control environment
   II. Control activities

(A) I only
(B) II only
(C) Both I and II
(D) Neither I nor II

69. Internal controls of all of a reporting entity's operating units and business functions is a primary concern of:
   I.   The entity's independent auditor
   II. The entity's management and those charged with governance

(A) I only
(B) II only
(C) Both I and II
(D) Neither I nor II

70. The auditor is likely to focus the assessment of control risk on the entity's:
   I.   Reporting controls
   II. Operational controls

(A) I only
(B) II only
(C) Both I and II
(D) Neither I nor II

71. The component of internal control that refers to adequate physical safe-guards and segregation of duties is known as:
    I. Control environment
    II. Risk assessment
    III. Control activities

    (A) II and III only
    (B) I and III only
    (C) III only
    (D) I, II, and III

72. An auditor generally tests the segregation of duties by:
    I. Personal inquiry and observation
    II. Analytical procedures
    III. Inspecting and recalculating

    (A) I only
    (B) II and III only
    (C) I and III only
    (D) I and II only

73. In the internal control stage, an independent auditor searches for control activities to:
    I. Determine whether the opportunities to allow any person to both perpetrate and conceal fraud are minimized
    II. Determine whether procedures and records concerning the safeguarding of assets are reliable

    (A) I only
    (B) II only
    (C) Both I and II
    (D) Neither I nor II

74. An entity's ongoing monitoring activities often include:
    I. The audit of the annual financial statements
    II. Reviewing the payroll cycle

    (A) I only
    (B) II only
    (C) Both I and II
    (D) Neither I nor II

75. An auditor gains an understanding of the client's attempt to keep internal controls up to date. This ongoing process of keeping controls effective:
  I. Refers to the monitoring component of internal control
  II. Is often performed by the internal audit function

(A) I only
(B) II only
(C) Both I and II
(D) Neither I nor II

76. Which of the following is NOT one of the five components of internal control?
  I.   Control activities
  II. Control group
  III. Control risk

(A) II only
(B) II and III only
(C) III only
(D) I and II only

77. Management's attitude toward aggressive financial reporting and its emphasis on meeting projected profit goals most likely would significantly influence an entity's control environment when:
  I.   Management is dominated by one individual who is also a shareholder
  II. A significant portion of management compensation is represented by stock options
  III. Those charged with governance are active in overseeing the entity's financial reporting policies

(A) I and III only
(B) II and III only
(C) I only
(D) I and II only

78. In an audit in conformity with GAAS, an auditor gains an understanding of the client's internal controls. At this stage, what needs to be understood?
  I. The design of the client's system
  II. Whether the controls have been placed in operation

(A) I only
(B) II only
(C) Both I and II
(D) Neither I nor II

79. In an audit in accordance with GAAS, as part of understanding internal control, an auditor is required to:
    I. Obtain knowledge about the operating effectiveness of internal control
    II. Ascertain whether internal controls have been implemented
    (A) I only
    (B) II only
    (C) Both I and II
    (D) Neither I nor II

80. Which of the following describes the auditor's ultimate purpose of assessing control risk?
    I. Evaluate the risk of financial statement misstatement
    II. Make recommendations regarding the five components of internal control
    (A) I only
    (B) II only
    (C) Both I and II
    (D) Neither I nor II

81. Assessing control risk at a low level most likely would involve:
    I. Identifying specific controls relevant to specific assertions
    II. Performing more extensive substantive tests than originally planned
    (A) I only
    (B) II only
    (C) Both I and II
    (D) Neither I nor II

82. When an auditor chooses the substantive approach and increases the assessed level of control risk because certain control activities were determined to be ineffective, the auditor would most likely:
    I. Increase the extent of tests of controls
    II. Increase the extent of substantive procedures
    (A) I only
    (B) II only
    (C) Both I and II
    (D) Neither I nor II

83. After gaining an understanding of a client's internal control, an auditor chose to use the combined approach to further audit procedures. Which of the following would be a reason that the auditor chose the combined approach?
  I. Based on the auditor's assessment of internal control, the auditor thinks the controls are in place.
  II. The auditor would choose the combined approach if testing controls would reduce further substantive procedures.

(A) I only
(B) II only
(C) Both I and II
(D) Neither I nor II

84. After gaining and documenting an understanding of the components of internal control, the auditor should make a preliminary assessment of control risk. If the auditor's investigation indicates that internal control is probably weak, the auditor should:
  I. Use the combined approach for further audit procedures
  II. Emphasize substantive testing rather than test of controls

(A) I only
(B) II only
(C) Both I and II
(D) Neither I nor II

85. An auditor must obtain an understanding of the components of a client's internal control. Auditors often choose to use questionnaires to gain information because:
  I. Each "no" response suggests a potential internal control weakness
  II. Compared to flowcharting, both strengths and weaknesses are easier to determine with a questionnaire

(A) I only
(B) II only
(C) Both I and II
(D) Neither I nor II

86. An auditor's flowchart of the accounting system is a diagrammatic representation that shows the auditor's:
  I. Understanding of the system
  II. Assessment of control risk

(A) I only
(B) II only
(C) Both I and II
(D) Neither I nor II

87. To obtain audit evidence about control risk, an auditor seeks to test controls and test for segregation of duties. The auditor will likely test for segregation of duties by:

    (A) Inquiry
    (B) Observation
    (C) Confirmations
    (D) Preparing a questionnaire or flowchart

88. An auditor is performing tests of controls in hopes of assessing control risk to be low in order to reduce overall audit testing. After obtaining an understanding of the design of an individual system, the auditor should:

    I. Seek to identify specific control activities within that system that would reduce control risk if they are operating effectively and efficiently, as intended
    II. Analyze and confirm

    (A) I only
    (B) II only
    (C) Both I and II
    (D) Neither I nor II

89. An auditor would test controls to gather evidence about:

    I. Whether a control is functioning as designed
    II. Whether an account balance is fairly stated

    (A) I only
    (B) II only
    (C) Both I and II
    (D) Neither I nor II

90. The auditor should design "further audit procedures" before the assessment of:

    I. Inherent risk
    II. Control risk

    (A) I only
    (B) II only
    (C) Both I and II
    (D) Neither I nor II

91. In an audit of financial statements, the entity's management is responsible for:

   I. Establishing, maintaining, and monitoring the entity's internal controls

  II. Considering whether those controls are operating as intended

(A) I only
(B) II only
(C) Both I and II
(D) Neither I nor II

92. With regard to automated controls and manual controls, an auditor would expect to find manual controls when:

   I. Judgment and discretion are required

  II. Large, nonrecurring transactions are involved

(A) I only
(B) II only
(C) Both I and II
(D) Neither I nor II

93. An auditor would expect to find manual controls rather than automated controls when:

   I. Potential misstatements are more difficult to predict

  II. Transactions are high volume and recurring

(A) I only
(B) II only
(C) Both I and II
(D) Neither I nor II

94. Which of the following represents an inherent limitation of internal control?

   I. Collusion among employees

  II. Mistakes in judgment

(A) I only
(B) II only
(C) Both I and II
(D) Neither I nor II

95. Which of the following represents an inherent limitation of internal control?
    I. Management override
    II. Incompatible duties
    (A) I only
    (B) II only
    (C) Both I and II
    (D) Neither I nor II

96. Under US GAAS, which of the following is always necessary in a financial statement audit?
    I. An indication whether or not the financial statements agree with the accounting records
    II. Risk assessment procedures
    III. Testing of controls
    (A) I, II, and III
    (B) I and III only
    (C) II and III only
    (D) I and II only

97. In an audit performed under GAAS, which of the following should an auditor do when control risk is assessed at the maximum level?
    (A) Perform fewer substantive tests of details.
    (B) Document the assessment.
    (C) Document the control structure more extensively.
    (D) Perform more tests of controls.

98. Tests of controls must be performed:
    I. When the auditor's risk assessment is based on the assumption that controls are operating effectively
    II. When substantive procedures alone are insufficient
    (A) I only
    (B) II only
    (C) Both I and II
    (D) Neither I nor II

CHAPTER 4

Audit Documentation, Related-Party Transactions, and Subsequent Events

99. An auditor maintains a current file within the audit documentation. This file should:

    I.   Contain all of the evidential material gathered to support the opinion rendered by the auditor

   II.   Contain a working trial balance

   (A) I only

   (B) II only

   (C) Both I and II

   (D) Neither I nor II

100. Which of the following would be maintained in the permanent file?

    I.   Copies of documents such as the reporting company's organization chart and long-term contracts

   II.   The audit plan and management representation letter

   (A) I only

   (B) II only

   (C) Both I and II

   (D) Neither I nor II

101. The permanent file most likely would include copies of the:

   (A) Auditor's lead schedules

   (B) Client attorney's letters

   (C) Client bank statements

   (D) Client debt agreements

102. The permanent file of an auditor's working papers would NOT include:
  I. Bond indenture agreements
  II. Lease agreements
  III. Lead schedules
  IV. Working trial balances

  (A) I and II only
  (B) II and III only
  (C) III only
  (D) III and IV only

103. No deletions of audit documentation are allowed after the:

  (A) Client's year-end
  (B) Documentation completion date
  (C) Last date of significant fieldwork
  (D) Report release date

104. Which of the following factors would likely affect an auditor's judgment about the quantity, type, and content of the auditor's working papers?
  I. The assessed level of control risk
  II. The type of audit report issued

  (A) I only
  (B) II only
  (C) Both I and II
  (D) Neither I nor II

105. Which of the following is NOT a primary function of audit working papers?

  (A) Assisting management in proving that the financial statements are in accordance with generally accepted accounting principles
  (B) Assisting the audit team members responsible for supervision in reviewing the work of the audit staff
  (C) Assisting auditors in planning engagements from one year to the next
  (D) Providing the auditor with support for the opinion that was rendered on the financial statements

106. Which of the following is correct concerning related-party transactions?

   I. The audit procedures directed toward identifying related-party transactions should include considering whether transactions are occurring but are not given proper accounting recognition.

  II. An auditor should substantiate that related-party transactions were consummated on terms equivalent to those that prevail in arm's-length transactions.

(A) I only
(B) II only
(C) Both I and II
(D) Neither I nor II

107. Which of the following auditing procedures most likely would assist an auditor in identifying related-party transactions?

   I. Searching accounting records for recurring transactions recorded just after the balance sheet date

  II. Reviewing confirmations of loans receivable and payable for indications of loan guarantees

(A) I only
(B) II only
(C) Both I and II
(D) Neither I nor II

108. X Company sells a significant amount of inventory to its affiliate, Y Company. They are separate companies but the same parent owns both. The amount of these sales must be included in the notes to the financial statements produced by:

   I. X Company

  II. Y Company

(A) I only
(B) II only
(C) Both I and II
(D) Neither I nor II

109. When investigating the possibility of related-party transactions, the auditor should look carefully for transactions that do not fit into patterns typically anticipated. Which of the following loans made by the client would make the auditor suspicious of a related-party loan?

   I. The loan was made without a fixed interest rate.

   II. The loan was made with no maturity date.

   III. The loan was made with a rate of interest that the auditor considers extremely low.

(A) I and II only

(B) I and III only

(C) I, II, and III

(D) II and III only

110. Just before the end of the year, a company sells several acres of land that had been held for a number of years. The sales price was significantly above the book value of the property so that a large gain was recognized. Neither this transaction nor any other transaction has been disclosed as a related-party transaction. Which of the following is correct?

   I. Since the sales price was significantly above the book value of the property, the auditor should be particularly suspicious that a related-party transaction has occurred.

   II. If the land had been sold involving an amount significantly different from its fair market value, the auditor likely would not suspect a related-party transaction.

(A) I only

(B) II only

(C) Both I and II

(D) Neither I nor II

111. Which of the following procedures would an auditor most likely perform to obtain evidence about the occurrence of subsequent events?

   I. Comparing the financial statements being reported on with those of the prior period

   II. Investigating personnel changes in the accounting department occurring after year-end

(A) I only

(B) II only

(C) Both I and II

(D) Neither I nor II

112. If the auditor believes that a client's financial statements need to be revised to reflect a subsequent event and management does not make the revision, the auditor should express which type of opinion?

(A) Unmodified with an other-matters paragraph
(B) Disclaimer or qualified
(C) Adverse or qualified
(D) Qualified or unmodified

113. Which of the following is correct regarding the auditor's responsibility for subsequent events?

I. The auditor has an active responsibility to make continuing inquiries between the date of the financial statements and the date of the auditor's report.

II. The auditor has an active responsibility to make continuing inquiries after the date of the auditor's report.

(A) I only
(B) II only
(C) Both I and II
(D) Neither I nor II

114. Which of the following statements is NOT true regarding the auditor's responsibility for subsequent events?

(A) The auditor has an active responsibility to make continuing inquiries between the date of the financial statements and the date on which sufficient appropriate audit evidence has been obtained.
(B) The auditor has an active responsibility to make continuing inquiries between the date of the financial statements and the date of the auditor's report.
(C) The auditor has an active responsibility to make continuing inquiries between the date of the auditor's report and the date on which the report is submitted.
(D) The auditor has no active responsibility to make continuing inquiries after the date of the auditor's report.

CHAPTER 5

Audit Reporting

115. For an audit of a nonissuer, which of the following paragraphs is found in a standard unmodified audit report?

   I. Scope
  II. Introductory
 III. Management's responsibility
 IV. Auditor's responsibility

  (A) I, II, III, and IV
  (B) III and IV only
  (C) I, II, and IV only
  (D) II, III, and IV only

116. How many paragraphs are found in a standard unmodified audit report?

  (A) 3
  (B) 4
  (C) 5
  (D) 6

117. Put these paragraphs in the order they appear in a standard unmodified audit report:

   I. Management's responsibility
  II. Auditor's responsibility
 III. Introductory
 IV. Opinion
  V. Scope

  (A) III, II, I, IV
  (B) III, V, I, II, IV
  (C) III, V, II, I, IV
  (D) III, I, II, IV

118. Under GAAS, in the auditor's responsibility paragraph, how does an auditor describe his or her responsibility regarding the client's internal controls?

    (A) Examined internal controls
    (B) Evaluated the overall internal controls
    (C) Expressed an opinion on internal controls
    (D) Considered internal controls

119. According to the opinion paragraph found in the standard unmodified audit report:

    I.   The auditor has assessed the accounting principles and evaluated significant accounting estimates used by the reporting entity
    II. "Present fairly" and US GAAP are specifically referenced

    (A) I only
    (B) II only
    (C) Both I and II
    (D) Neither I nor II

120. The auditor's standard report implies that the auditor is satisfied that the comparability of financial statements between periods:

    I.   Has not been materially affected by changes in accounting principles
    II. Has been consistently applied between or among periods

    (A) I only
    (B) II only
    (C) Both I and II
    (D) Neither I nor II

121. An emphasis-of-matter paragraph is included in the auditor's report:

    I.   When required by GAAS
    II. At the auditor's discretion

    (A) I only
    (B) II only
    (C) Both I and II
    (D) Neither I nor II

122. The inclusion of an emphasis-of-matter paragraph in the auditor's report:

    I.   Is used when referring to a matter that is not appropriately presented in the financial statements
    II. Does not affect the auditor's opinion

    (A) I only
    (B) II only
    (C) Both I and II
    (D) Neither I nor II

123. Which of the following is correct regarding the adding of an emphasis-of-matter paragraph to an unmodified report?

    I. If the auditor decides to add a paragraph, the extra paragraph should go before the opinion paragraph.

    II. The emphasis paragraph should contain a statement that the auditor's opinion may need to be modified.

(A) I only

(B) II only

(C) Both I and II

(D) Neither I nor II

124. An other-matters paragraph is used:

    I. When required by GAAS

    II. At the auditor's discretion

(A) I only

(B) II only

(C) Both I and II

(D) Neither I nor II

125. Other-matters paragraphs refer to matters that are relevant to the user's understanding of the:

    I. Financial statements

    II. Auditor's responsibilities

    III. Auditor's report

(A) II and III only

(B) II only

(C) I and II only

(D) I, II, and III

126. An auditor would express an unmodified opinion with an emphasis-of-matter paragraph added to the auditor's report for a:

    I. Justified change in accounting principle

    II. Material internal control weakness

(A) I only

(B) II only

(C) Both I and II

(D) Neither I nor II

127. The preparation and fair presentation of the financial statements requires:
    I. Identification of the applicable financial reporting framework
    II. Inclusion of an adequate description of the framework

    (A) I only
    (B) II only
    (C) Both I and II
    (D) Neither I nor II

128. If an auditor chooses an emphasis-of-matter paragraph to describe a going concern issue, which of the following is required language in that emphasis paragraph?
    I. "12 months from the balance sheet date"
    II. "Reasonable period of time"

    (A) I only
    (B) II only
    (C) Both I and II
    (D) Neither I nor II

129. Where does a group auditor make reference to a component auditor in a division of responsibility?
    I. Emphasis-of-matter paragraph
    II. Other-matters paragraph

    (A) I only
    (B) II only
    (C) Both I and II
    (D) Neither I nor II

130. When a group auditor decides to make reference to the examination of a component auditor:
    I. The group auditor's report should not make reference to the "component auditor" in the auditor's responsibility paragraph
    II. The introductory paragraph is the same whether the auditor divides responsibility or not

    (A) I only
    (B) II only
    (C) Both I and II
    (D) Neither I nor II

131. A typical auditor's report should include a reference to the country of origin of:
   I. The auditing standards the auditor followed in performing the audit
   II. The accounting principles used to prepare the financial statements

(A) I only
(B) II only
(C) Both I and II
(D) Neither I nor II

132. An auditor can issue an unmodified report without any reference to consistency when:
   I. The client changes from straight line depreciation to accelerated depreciation
   II. The client changes the useful life of an asset used to calculate depreciation expense

(A) I only
(B) II only
(C) Both I and II
(D) Neither I nor II

133. A group auditor chose to divide the responsibility for an audit with another firm. This other firm issued a qualified opinion on the financial statements of the subsidiaries that it audited. Which of the following is correct regarding the responsibility of the group auditor?
   I. The group auditor must render a qualified opinion on the consolidated financial statements.
   II. The group auditor may not render an unmodified opinion on the consolidated financial statements.

(A) I only
(B) II only
(C) Both I and II
(D) Neither I nor II

134. Which of the following correctly describes the effect on the auditor's otherwise unmodified report when a client changes an accounting principle that has a material effect on the financial statements but the auditor concurs with the change?

    I. An emphasis-of-matter paragraph preceding the opinion paragraph is required.

    II. If the previous accounting principle was NOT in conformity with GAAP, the emphasis-of-matter paragraph would still be required.

(A) I only
(B) II only
(C) Both I and II
(D) Neither I nor II

135. When an auditor qualifies an opinion because of a scope limitation, the wording in the opinion paragraph should indicate that the qualification pertains to:

    I. The possible effects on the financial statements
    II. The scope limitation itself

(A) I only
(B) II only
(C) Both I and II
(D) Neither I nor II

136. An auditor may issue a report that omits any reference to consistency when:

    I. The client changes from straight line to accelerated depreciation for property, plant, and equipment

    II. There is a change from an accounting principle that is NOT generally accepted to one that is generally accepted

(A) I only
(B) II only
(C) Both I and II
(D) Neither I nor II

137. If a publicly held company issues financial statements that purport to present its financial position and results of operations but omits the statement of cash flows, the auditor ordinarily will express:

(A) An unmodified opinion with an emphasis-of-matter paragraph
(B) A qualified opinion
(C) An unmodified opinion without an emphasis-of-matter paragraph
(D) A disclaimer of qualified opinion

138. When an auditor expresses an adverse opinion, the opinion paragraph should include:

   I. The substantive reasons for the financial statements being misleading

   II. A direct reference to a separate paragraph disclosing the basis for the opinion

(A) I only

(B) II only

(C) Both I and II

(D) Neither I nor II

139. An auditor would NOT issue a disclaimer of opinion for:

   I. Inadequate disclosure

   II. An accounting principle change that the auditor does not agree with

(A) I only

(B) II only

(C) Both I and II

(D) Neither I nor II

140. After performing an audit, the independent CPA is still somewhat concerned that the financial statements are not free from all material misstatements. If, in the auditor's judgment, the misstatements were material but not pervasive, the opinion expressed is likely to be:

(A) Unmodified

(B) Adverse

(C) Disclaimer

(D) Qualified

141. When an auditor expresses a qualified opinion due to a material misstatement of the financial statements, the auditor's responsibility paragraph should be amended to state that the auditor believes that the audit evidence obtained is sufficient and appropriate to provide a basis for the auditor's:

(A) Opinion

(B) Modified opinion

(C) Qualified opinion

(D) Nonstandard opinion

142. Which of the following is an implicit representation when issuing the auditor's report on comparative financial statements under US auditing standards?
     I. Obtaining evidence that is sufficient and appropriate
     II. Consistent application of accounting principles

     (A) I only
     (B) II only
     (C) Both I and II
     (D) Neither I nor II

143. An auditor who is unable to form an opinion on a new client's opening inventory balances may NOT issue an unmodified opinion on the current year's:
     I. Balance sheet
     II. Income statement
     III. Statement of cash flows

     (A) I and III only
     (B) I only
     (C) III only
     (D) II and III only

144. When an auditor issues an adverse opinion or disclaimer on the financial statements taken as a whole, the auditor could still issue an unmodified opinion on just:
     I. The income statement
     II. Property, plant, and equipment

     (A) I only
     (B) II only
     (C) Both I and II
     (D) Neither I nor II

CHAPTER 6

Reviews and Compilations

145. SSARS applies to:

    (A) Compilations but not reviews
    (B) Reviews but not compilations
    (C) Compilations and reviews of publicly traded companies
    (D) Compilations and reviews of non-publicly traded companies

146. Which of the following audit procedures generally is NOT performed in a review engagement?

    I. Going concern
    II. Inquiries of the entity's outside legal counsel

    (A) I only
    (B) II only
    (C) Both I and II
    (D) Neither I nor II

147. Which of the following documentation would likely NOT be included in a review engagement of a nonissuer?

    I. Procedures used to assess control risk
    II. Inquiring about subsequent events

    (A) I only
    (B) II only
    (C) Both I and II
    (D) Neither I nor II

148. Which of the following procedures is likely to be performed in a compilation?

    I. Analytical procedures
    II. Inquiries

    (A) I only
    (B) II only
    (C) Both I and II
    (D) Neither I nor II

149. An accountant compiles unaudited financial statements that are NOT expected to be used by a third party. The accountant may decline to issue a compilation report provided:
    I. A written representation letter is obtained from the client's management
    II. A written engagement letter is used to document the understanding with the client
    (A) I only
    (B) II only
    (C) Both I and II
    (D) Neither I nor II

150. An accountant who had begun a review of the financial statements of a nonissuer was asked to change the engagement to a compilation. If there is reasonable justification for the change, the accountant's report should include reference to the:
    I. Reason for the change
    II. Original engagement that was agreed to
    (A) I only
    (B) II only
    (C) Both I and II
    (D) Neither I nor II

151. If requested to perform a review engagement for a nonissuer in which an accountant has an immaterial direct financial interest, the accountant is:
    (A) Not independent and, therefore, may not issue a compilation
    (B) Not independent and, therefore, may not issue a review report, but may issue a compilation
    (C) Not independent and, therefore, may not be associated with the financial statements
    (D) Independent because the financial interest is immaterial and, therefore, may issue a review report

152. A review provides limited assurance that there are no material modifications that should be made to the financial statements in order for them to be in conformity with generally accepted accounting principles, whereas a compilation:
    (A) Provides limited assurance that the CPA followed SSARS and the client followed GAAP
    (B) Provides negative assurance that no material modifications need to be made to the financial statements, rather than reasonable assurance
    (C) Provides negative assurance that no material modifications need to be made to the financial statements, rather than limited assurance
    (D) Provides no assurance

153. Which of the following types of engagements tests for reasonableness of the financial statements?
  I. Compilations
  II. Reviews

(A) I only
(B) II only
(C) Both I and II
(D) Neither I nor II

154. If independence is compromised:

(A) The CPA can still express limited assurance on the financial statements
(B) The CPA can still perform a compilation engagement
(C) Disclosing such lack of independence would not compensate for the lack of independence and, therefore, the CPA would need to withdraw from a compilation engagement
(D) None of the above

155. A review for a nonissuer that is prepared unmodified from the standard review report will contain how many paragraphs?

(A) 4
(B) 5
(C) 2
(D) 3

156. In a standard unmodified review report for a nonissuer, the second paragraph is known as the:

(A) Opinion paragraph
(B) CPA's responsibility paragraph
(C) Scope paragraph
(D) Management responsibility paragraph

157. As part of the CPA's responsibilities in performing a review engagement for a nonissuer, which of the following is required evidence to be signed by the client?
  I. Engagement letter
  II. Management representation letter

(A) I only
(B) II only
(C) Both I and II
(D) Neither I nor II

158. As part of the CPA's responsibilities in performing a compilation, which of the following is required evidence to be signed by the client?
I. Engagement letter
II. Management representation letter
(A) I only
(B) II only
(C) Both I and II
(D) Neither I nor II

159. In which of the following engagements are analytical procedures carried out?

	Review	Compilation
(A)	Yes	Yes
(B)	No	No
(C)	Yes	No
(D)	No	Yes

160. A standard compilation report on historical financial statements prepared with footnotes by an independent CPA contains how many paragraphs?
(A) 3
(B) 4
(C) 5
(D) 2

161. A compilation report presented without footnotes by a CPA who is NOT independent:
(A) Cannot be performed because the CPA is not independent
(B) Cannot be performed because the CPA lacks independence and the report lacks disclosures required under GAAP
(C) Can be performed if the client is not a relative of the CPA and all instances of a lack of independence are provided
(D) Can be performed provided the report discloses both the lack of independence and the fact that the disclosures are missing

162. How many paragraphs are found in the following standard reports for a nonissuer?

	Review	Compilation
(A)	4	4
(B)	2	3
(C)	4	3
(D)	2	4

163. Which of the following ordinarily applies to both a review and a compilation engagement for a nonissuer?
   I. Distribution of report is restricted
  II. Engagement letter is required
 III. Analytical procedures and inquiries are performed

(A) I, II, and III
(B) III only
(C) II only
(D) I and II only

164. Which of the following engagements provided by a CPA to a nonissuer requires the CPA to be independent even though no opinion will be expressed?
   I. Review engagements
  II. Compilations of financial statements that include footnotes

(A) I only
(B) II only
(C) Both I and II
(D) Neither I nor II

165. Which of the following engagements requires the CPA to be independent even though no assurance is being provided?
   I. Review engagements of a nonpublic entity
  II. Compilation engagements

(A) I only
(B) II only
(C) Both I and II
(D) Neither I nor II

CHAPTER 7

Reporting on Special Purpose Frameworks and Other Reporting Issues

166. Reports on special purpose frameworks are issued in conjunction with:
    I. Cash basis
    II. Income tax basis
    III. Regulatory basis of accounting

    (A) I and III only
    (B) I and II only
    (C) II and III only
    (D) I, II, and III

167. An auditor's report will contain an emphasis-of-matter paragraph alerting readers to a special purpose framework when the financial statements are prepared using the:
    I. Income tax basis
    II. Cash basis

    (A) I only
    (B) II only
    (C) Both I and II
    (D) Neither I nor II

168. When a CPA reports on financial statements prepared on the cash basis:
    I. The report will contain an emphasis-of-matter paragraph
    II. The opinion paragraph will evaluate the usefulness of the basis of accounting and compare it to GAAP

    (A) I only
    (B) II only
    (C) Both I and II
    (D) Neither I nor II

169. A report on special purpose framework financial statements prepared on the income tax basis should include an emphasis-of-matter paragraph:
  I. Stating the basis of accounting used
  II. Referring to the footnote in the financial statements that describes the basis of accounting
  III. Indicating that it is a non-GAAP basis

  (A) I only
  (B) I, II, and III
  (C) I and III only
  (D) II and III only

170. Which of the following reports would contain restricted use language?
  I. A report on a client's compliance with a regulatory requirement, assuming the report is prepared based on a financial statement audit of the complete financial statements
  II. A report on financial statements prepared on the cash basis of accounting

  (A) I only
  (B) II only
  (C) Both I and II
  (D) Neither I nor II

171. An auditor's report on special purpose financial statements will contain a restricted use paragraph (other matters) when the financial statements are presented using the:
  I. Cash basis
  II. Income tax basis

  (A) I only
  (B) II only
  (C) Both I and II
  (D) Neither I nor II

172. Which of the following will be included in an auditor's report on special purpose financial statements NOT intended for general use?
  I. Emphasis-of-matter paragraph alerting the reader about the preparation in accordance with a special purpose framework
  II. Other-matters paragraph restricting the use of the auditor's report

  (A) I only
  (B) II only
  (C) Both I and II
  (D) Neither I nor II

173. A dual opinion on special purpose frameworks and GAAP would be required if the financial statements were prepared on which of the following frameworks?

    I. Income tax basis

  II. Cash basis

(A) I only

(B) II only

(C) Both I and II

(D) Neither I nor II

174. A CPA is asked to report on one financial statement and not the others. The auditor should do which of the following?

(A) Accept the engagement but disclaim an opinion because the complete set of financial statements was not audited

(B) Not accept the engagement because it would constitute a violation of the profession's ethical standards

(C) Not accept the engagement because reporting on one financial statement and not the others is not permitted unless the auditor is not independent

(D) Accept the engagement because such engagements merely involve special considerations in the application of US GAAS

175. Clyde, CPA, has been asked to report on the balance sheet of Western Company but not on the other basic financial statements. Which of the following is required of Clyde?

    I. When auditing a single financial statement, Clyde should perform procedures, as necessary, on interrelated items (sales/receivables, inventory/payables, fixed assets/depreciation).

  II. When auditing a single financial statement, Clyde may perform the audit as a separate engagement or in conjunction with an audit of an entity's complete set of financial statements.

(A) I only

(B) II only

(C) Both I and II

(D) Neither I nor II

176. Clyde, CPA, has been asked to report on the balance sheet of Western Company but not on the other basic financial statements. Which of the following is required of Clyde?

   I. When auditing a single financial statement, the auditor should determine materiality for the complete set of financial statements rather than for the single financial statement.

  II. When auditing a single financial statement, the auditor should obtain an understanding of the intended users of the statement.

(A) I only
(B) II only
(C) Both I and II
(D) Neither I nor II

177. Starkey, CPA, expressed an adverse opinion on the financial statements of Harrison Corp. Which of the following is required if Starkey wishes to express an unmodified opinion on a specific element of those financial statements?

   I. The specific element must not be a major part of the total financial statements.

  II. The report on the specific element must be shown together with the report on the complete financial statements.

(A) I only
(B) II only
(C) Both I and II
(D) Neither I nor II

178. Which of the following is correct with regard to an auditor's report on compliance?

   I. An auditor's report would be designated a report on compliance when it is issued in connection with compliance with aspects of regulatory requirements related to audited financial statements.

  II. An auditor's report on compliance does not involve the auditor giving positive assurance regarding compliance with regulatory requirements.

(A) I only
(B) II only
(C) Both I and II
(D) Neither I nor II

179. Which of the following is correct regarding an auditor's report on compliance?

    I. The auditor does not have to audit the client's complete financial statements in order to issue a report on compliance.

    II. The report on compliance could express positive or negative assurance on compliance.

(A) I only
(B) II only
(C) Both I and II
(D) Neither I nor II

180. Which of the following is correct regarding an auditor's report on compliance?

    I. Would contain negative assurance if material instances of noncompliance were discovered by the auditor

    II. Would express negative assurance if the auditor issued a disclaimer or adverse opinion on the complete financial statements

(A) I only
(B) II only
(C) Both I and II
(D) Neither I nor II

181. The auditor's report on compliance with a regulatory requirement:

    I. Must be a separate report from the auditor's report on the financial statements

    II. Contains a paragraph restricting the use of the report

(A) I only
(B) II only
(C) Both I and II
(D) Neither I nor II

182. An auditor's report on compliance would include a restriction of use if the report on compliance was:

    I. Issued separately from the report on the financial statements

    II. Included as an other-matters paragraph in a report on the complete financial statements

(A) I only
(B) II only
(C) Both I and II
(D) Neither I nor II

183. An auditor's report on compliance may contain negative assurance regarding instances of noncompliance when:
    I. The auditor's report on compliance is issued separately from the report on the complete financial statements
    II. The auditor's report on compliance is issued as an other-matters paragraph within the auditor's report on complete financial statements
    (A) I only
    (B) II only
    (C) Both I and II
    (D) Neither I nor II

184. Which is correct regarding the auditor's report on compliance issued as a separate report from the auditor's report on the complete financial statements?
    I. The date of the separate report should be later than the auditor's report on the complete financial statements.
    II. The separate report should contain a statement that the audit was not directed primarily toward obtaining knowledge regarding compliance.
    (A) I only
    (B) II only
    (C) Both I and II
    (D) Neither I nor II

185. An auditor's standard report on compliance issued as a separate report would contain how many paragraphs?
    (A) 2
    (B) 3
    (C) 4
    (D) 5

186. Reports on special purpose frameworks, also known as special reports, include auditor's reports on:
    I. Compliance with reporting requirements to be filed with a specific regulatory agency
    II. Cash basis financial statements
    (A) I only
    (B) II only
    (C) Both I and II
    (D) Neither I nor II

187. Which of the following special reports provides negative assurance?
    I. Report on cash basis financial statements
    II. Auditor's report on compliance with aspects of contractual agreements
    (A) I only
    (B) II only
    (C) Both I and II
    (D) Neither I nor II

188. If there are both emphasis-of-matter and other-matters paragraphs in an auditor's report, in what order should the various paragraphs be presented?
    (A) Opinion paragraph, emphasis-of-matter paragraph, other-matters paragraph
    (B) Emphasis-of-matter paragraph, other-matters paragraph, opinion paragraph
    (C) Emphasis-of-matter paragraph, opinion paragraph, other-matters paragraph
    (D) Opinion paragraph, other-matters paragraph, emphasis-of-matter paragraph

189. An auditor may report on summary financial statements that are derived from complete financial statements if the auditor:
    I. Indicates in the report whether the information in the summary financial statements is fairly stated in all material respects in relation to the complete financial statements from which it has been derived
    II. Includes both the date of the report on the complete financial statements and the opinion expressed on those statements
    (A) I only
    (B) II only
    (C) Both I and II
    (D) Neither I nor II

190. Which of the following engagements should the auditor NOT accept unless the auditor also is engaged to audit the complete financial statements?
    I. Report on compliance with a regulatory requirement
    II. Report on summary financial statements
    (A) I only
    (B) II only
    (C) Both I and II
    (D) Neither I nor II

191. When an entity is required by the SEC to file a quarterly report:
    I. An independent accountant must perform an audit of the interim financial information before the quarterly report is filed
    II. The CPA must follow PCAOB standards

    (A) I only
    (B) II only
    (C) Both I and II
    (D) Neither I nor II

192. Regarding fraud, as part of a review of interim financial information for a public entity, the accountant is required to inquire of management about its knowledge of:
    I. Suspected fraud
    II. Allegations of fraud

    (A) I only
    (B) II only
    (C) Both I and II
    (D) Neither I nor II

193. Andriola, CPA, has been hired to perform an interim review of Prager Corp., an issuer. In a review on interim financial information for a public entity, Andriola's knowledge about Prager Corp.'s business and its internal control would influence Andriola's:
    I. Inquiries
    II. Analytical procedures performed
    III. Timing of inventory observation

    (A) I, II, and III
    (B) II only
    (C) I only
    (D) I and II only

194. The annual financial statements of Hosana Inc., a publicly held company, have been audited and its interim financial statements have been reviewed. Both engagements were performed by Adams, Franklin, and Dickinson, CPAs. Which of the following is true about the application of professional standards to this review?
    I. Statements on Standards for Accounting and Review Services apply.
    II. PCAOB standards apply.

    (A) I only
    (B) II only
    (C) Both I and II
    (D) Neither I nor II

195. Which of the following is a required procedure in an engagement to review the interim financial information of a publicly held entity?

   I. Obtaining corroborating evidence about the entity's ability to continue as a going concern

   II. Inquiries of management about their knowledge of fraud or suspected fraud

   (A) I only

   (B) II only

   (C) Both I and II

   (D) Neither I nor II

196. Which of the following is an example of disaggregated data that a CPA is required to compare in a review of interim financial information for an issuer?

   I. Disaggregated revenue data for the current interim period with that of comparable prior periods

   II. Disaggregated revenue data for the entity with that of competitors in the industry

   (A) I only

   (B) II only

   (C) Both I and II

   (D) Neither I nor II

197. Salt, CPA, is performing an interim review of quarterly financial information of Peter Corp., an issuer. Inquiries of which of the following is required by Salt?

   I. Peter Corp.'s management

   II. Peter Corp.'s outside legal counsel

   (A) I only

   (B) II only

   (C) Both I and II

   (D) Neither I nor II

198. Which of the following procedures is required in a review of interim financial statements of an issuer?

   I. Inquiry regarding compliance with GAAP

   II. Management representation letter

   III. Engagement letter

   (A) I and II only

   (B) II and III only

   (C) I and III only

   (D) I, II, and III

199. Boyle Inc. is an issuer. Tanner, CPA, is performing a review of Boyle's interim financial information. As part of planning, Tanner reads the audit documentation from the preceding year's annual audit. Which of the following is likely to affect Tanner's review?
    I. Identified risks of material misstatement due to fraud
   II. Scope limitations that were overcome through acceptable alternative procedures

  (A) I only
  (B) II only
  (C) Both I and II
  (D) Neither I nor II

200. Which of the following is correct regarding a comfort letter?
    I. A comfort letter contains a restriction on the use of the report.
   II. In a comfort letter, negative assurance is provided on unaudited financial information.

  (A) I only
  (B) II only
  (C) Both I and II
  (D) Neither I nor II

CHAPTER 8

Attestation Engagements Other than Audits of Historic Financial Information

201. Which of the following is correct regarding attestation standards?
   I. Sufficient evidence shall be obtained to provide a reasonable basis for the conclusion that is expressed in the report.
   II. The work shall be adequately planned, and assistants, if any, shall be properly supervised.
   III. A sufficient understanding of internal control shall be obtained to plan the engagement.

   (A) I and III only
   (B) II and III only
   (C) II only
   (D) I and II only

202. Which of the following is an essential principle of a trust engagement?
   I. Processing integrity
   II. Online privacy
   III. Confidentiallty

   (A) I and II only
   (B) II and III only
   (C) I and III only
   (D) I, II, and III

203. A CPA reporting on which of the following types of trust engagements would need to follow Statements on Standards for Attestation Engagements (SSAE)?

   I. SysTrusts

  II. WebTrusts

(A) I only

(B) II only

(C) Both I and II

(D) Neither I nor II

204. Which of the following attestation engagements may a CPA perform that would allow the client to affix a seal of approval on the client's Internet site indicating, among other things, transaction integrity?

(A) WebGem

(B) WebTrust

(C) WebSys

(D) SysWeb

205. Statements on Standards for Attestation Engagements (SSAE) do NOT apply to:

   I. Pro forma financial statements

  II. Tax preparation services

(A) I only

(B) II only

(C) Both I and II

(D) Neither I nor II

206. Statements on Standards for Attestation Engagements (SSAE) do NOT apply to reports and services relating to:

   I. Forecasts

  II. Projections

(A) I only

(B) II only

(C) Both I and II

(D) Neither I nor II

207. Statements on Standards for Attestation Engagements do NOT apply to:

   I. Audits of nonissuers

  II. Compilations

 III. Reviews of nonissuers

(A) I only

(B) II and III only

(C) II only

(D) I, II, and III

208. Which of the following is generally correct regarding an agreed-upon procedures engagement?

    I. Agreed-upon procedures engagements follow Statements on Stan-
dards for Agreed-Upon Procedures.

    II. The CPA need not be independent if the client chooses the proce-
dures for the CPA to report on.

(A) I only
(B) II only
(C) Both I and II
(D) Neither I nor II

209. Which of the following is correct regarding agreed-upon procedures
engagements?

    I. The CPA's report is limited in distribution.

    II. The CPA takes responsibility for the adequacy of the procedures
selected.

(A) I only
(B) II only
(C) Both I and II
(D) Neither I nor II

210. In an agreed-upon procedures engagement, which of the following is
correct?

    I. The CPA provides negative assurance in the report.

    II. The report is restricted in distribution.

(A) I only
(B) II only
(C) Both I and II
(D) Neither I nor II

211. Which of the following engagements requires the CPA to be independent
even though no assurance is being provided?

    I. Review engagements of a nonpublic entity

    II. Agreed-upon procedures engagements

(A) I only
(B) II only
(C) Both I and II
(D) Neither I nor II

212. Which of the following engagements requires the CPA to be independent even though no opinion is being expressed?
    I. Review engagements of a nonpublic entity
   II. Agreed-upon procedures engagements

(A) I only
(B) II only
(C) Both I and II
(D) Neither I nor II

213. An examination of a financial forecast is a professional service that involves:
    I. Assembling and compiling a financial forecast that is based on management's assumptions
   II. Evaluating the preparation of a financial forecast and the support underlying management's assumptions

(A) I only
(B) II only
(C) Both I and II
(D) Neither I nor II

214. An accountant's report on a financial forecast should include a caveat that the prospective results of the financial forecast may NOT be achieved if the accountant:
    I. Performed agreed-upon procedures regarding the client's forecast
   II. Reviewed the client's forecast

(A) I only
(B) II only
(C) Both I and II
(D) Neither I nor II

215. A CPA in public practice is required to comply with the provisions of the Statements on Standards for Attestation Engagements (SSAE) when:
    I. Compiling a client's financial projection that presents a hypothetical course of action
   II. Compiling a client's historical financial statements

(A) I only
(B) II only
(C) Both I and II
(D) Neither I nor II

216. In an attest engagement, use of the accountant's report should be restricted to specified parties:
 I. When reporting directly on the subject matter and a written assertion has not been provided
 II. When reporting on an agreed-upon procedures engagement

(A) I only
(B) II only
(C) Both I and II
(D) Neither I nor II

217. In an attestation engagement where the CPA examines and reports directly on subject matter, which of the following phrases would likely be in the report?
 I. "We have examined management's assertion"
 II. "We have examined the accompanying schedule"

(A) I only
(B) II only
(C) Both I and II
(D) Neither I nor II

218. Negative assurance may be expressed when an accountant reports on:
 I. Compilation of prospective financial statements
 II. Results of performing a review of management's assertion

(A) I only
(B) II only
(C) Both I and II
(D) Neither I nor II

219. Which of the following items should be included in prospective financial statements issued in an attestation engagement performed in accordance with Statements on Standards for Attestation Engagements?
 I. All significant assumptions used to prepare the financial statements
 II. Historical financial statements for the past three years

(A) I only
(B) II only
(C) Both I and II
(D) Neither I nor II

220. SSAE standards do NOT apply to reports and services relating to:
   I. Internal control
   II. Consulting

(A) I only
(B) II only
(C) Both I and II
(D) Neither I nor II

221. An accountant's report on a financial forecast should include a caveat that the prospective results of the financial forecast may NOT be achieved if the accountant:
   I. Examined the client's forecast
   II. Compiled the client's forecast

(A) I only
(B) II only
(C) Both I and II
(D) Neither I nor II

222. An accountant's report on a financial forecast should include:
   I. A restriction in distribution
   II. A limitation on the usefulness of the report

(A) I only
(B) II only
(C) Both I and II
(D) Neither I nor II

223. An auditor's letter issued on significant deficiencies relating to a nonissuer's internal control observed during a financial statement audit should:
   I. Include a restriction on distribution
   II. Indicate that the purpose of the audit was to report on the financial statements and report on internal control

(A) I only
(B) II only
(C) Both I and II
(D) Neither I nor II

224. Significant deficiencies in internal control noted during a financial statement audit should be communicated to:
   I. Management
   II. Those charged with governance

(A) I only
(B) II only
(C) Both I and II
(D) Neither I nor II

225. Management provides an assertion concerning the effectiveness of internal control as part of a financial statement audit of:
   I. A nonissuer
   II. An issuer
   (A) I only
   (B) II only
   (C) Both I and II
   (D) Neither I nor II

226. Which of the following is correct regarding a practitioner's examination and report on management's assertion about the effectiveness of the entity's internal control?
   I. The examination must be integrated with an audit of the entity's financial statements.
   II. The practitioner's report must be limited in distribution.
   (A) I only
   (B) II only
   (C) Both I and II
   (D) Neither I nor II

227. Clark is a CPA whose clients are nonissuers. Which of the following reports issued by Clark must be limited in distribution?
   I. A report on significant deficiencies in internal control noted during a financial statement audit
   II. A report on the examination of a client's assertion about the effectiveness of the entity's internal control
   (A) I only
   (B) II only
   (C) Both I and II
   (D) Neither I nor II

228. In the audit of a nonissuer, which of the following is required to assess and report on internal control?
   I. Management
   II. The independent auditor
   (A) I only
   (B) II only
   (C) Both I and II
   (D) Neither I nor II

229. Which of the following is an appropriate topic regarding an auditor's communication to those charged with governance?
    I. The fact that no material weaknesses were noted in internal control that would affect the financial statements
    II. The fact that a material misstatement was noted by the auditor on the financial statements and corrected by management
    (A) I only
    (B) II only
    (C) Both I and II
    (D) Neither I nor II

230. The auditor should ensure that those charged with governance are informed about:
    I. The basis for the auditor's conclusions regarding the reasonableness of sensitive accounting estimates
    II. Disagreements with management in the application of accounting principles relating to asset impairment
    (A) I only
    (B) II only
    (C) Both I and II
    (D) Neither I nor II

CHAPTER 9

Assertions

231. Which of the following is a financial statement assertion regarding classes of transactions?

    I. Completeness

   II. Occurrence

(A) I only

(B) II only

(C) Both I and II

(D) Neither I nor II

232. Which of the following is an assertion under the category of classes of transactions?

    I. Cutoff

   II. Completeness

  III. Occurrence

(A) II and III only

(B) I only

(C) I and III only

(D) I, II, and III

233. Within the assertion category known as classes of transactions, the cutoff assertion has a direct impact on which other assertions in that class?

    I. Completeness

   II. Occurrence

(A) I only

(B) II only

(C) Both I and II

(D) Neither I nor II

234. Which of the following is an assertion under the category of classes of transactions?
    I. Classification
    II. Accuracy
    III. Completeness
    (A) III only
    (B) I, II, and III
    (C) II and III only
    (D) I and III only

235. Which of the following is a financial statement assertion regarding account balances?
    I. Rights and obligations
    II. Valuation
    III. Existence
    (A) I and II only
    (B) I, II, and III
    (C) II and III only
    (D) III only

236. Which of the following is an assertion found under the category of account balances (balance sheet assertions)?
    I. Completeness
    II. Rights and obligations
    III. Existence
    IV. Valuation
    (A) II, III, and IV only
    (B) II and IV only
    (C) III and IV only
    (D) I, II, III, and IV

237. Accounts receivable affects one or more assertions. Which of the following assertions relates to accounts receivable?
    I. Existence
    II. Valuation
    III. Rights and obligations
    (A) I, II, and III
    (B) II and III only
    (C) I and II only
    (D) I and III only

238. Accounts receivable affects one or more assertions. Which of the following assertions relates to accounts receivable, net of allowance for doubtful accounts?
   I. Existence
   II. Valuation

(A) I only
(B) II only
(C) Both I and II
(D) Neither I nor II

239. Inventory that was bought right before the end of Year 1 was incorrectly recorded in Year 2 (the subsequent period). Which assertion is affected in Year 1?
   I. Completeness
   II. Existence

(A) I only
(B) II only
(C) Both I and II
(D) Neither I nor II

240. Completeness is an assertion found under the category of:
   I. Classes of transactions
   II. Account balances

(A) I only
(B) II only
(C) Both I and II
(D) Neither I nor II

241. Rights and obligations is an assertion found under the category of:
   I. Classes of transactions and events
   II. Account balances

(A) I only
(B) II only
(C) Both I and II
(D) Neither I nor II

242. Nadasky is the president of Johnson Corp. Karl is the auditor for Johnson Corp. Which assertion regarding account balances is affected if a debt owed by Nadasky was inappropriately reported on the balance sheet of Johnson Corp.?
   I. Completeness
   II. Rights and obligations

(A) I only
(B) II only
(C) Both I and II
(D) Neither I nor II

243. Nadasky is the president of Johnson Corp. Karl is the auditor for Johnson Corp. Which assertion regarding account balances is affected if a debt owed by Nadasky was inappropriately reported on the balance sheet of Johnson Corp.?
     I. Existence
     II. Rights and obligations

     (A) I only
     (B) II only
     (C) Both I and II
     (D) Neither I nor II

244. Nadasky is the president of Johnson Corp. Karl is the auditor for Johnson Corp. Which assertion regarding account balances is affected if a debt owed by the company is overstated on the balance sheet?
     I. Rights and obligations
     II. Completeness

     (A) I only
     (B) II only
     (C) Both I and II
     (D) Neither I nor II

245. Nadasky is the president of Johnson Corp. Karl is the auditor for Johnson Corp. Which assertion regarding account balances is affected if the accounting department of Johnson Corp. failed to record a company debt because it thought the debt was that of Nadasky?
     I. Completeness
     II. Existence

     (A) I only
     (B) II only
     (C) Both I and II
     (D) Neither I nor II

246. Luke, CPA, is the independent auditor for Nazareth Corp. Analee is the president of Nazareth Corp. Luke has decided that inventory is based on a variation of FIFO and LIFO that is not viewed as proper accounting according to US GAAP. Which assertion is impacted?
     I. Rights and obligations
     II. Valuation

     (A) I only
     (B) II only
     (C) Both I and II
     (D) Neither I nor II

247. The auditor has determined that inventory is overstated based on incorrect cutoff and a variation of FIFO and LIFO that is not viewed as proper accounting according to US GAAP. Which assertion is affected?
    I. Completeness
    II. Valuation
    (A) I only
    (B) II only
    (C) Both I and II
    (D) Neither I nor II

248. If inventory is understated based on incorrect cutoff and a variation of FIFO and LIFO that is not viewed as proper accounting according to US GAAP, which assertion is affected?
    I. Completeness
    II. Valuation
    (A) I only
    (B) II only
    (C) Both I and II
    (D) Neither I nor II

249. The reporting company records sales revenue and accounts receivable near the end of the year because a sales order has been received. However, the earnings process will not be complete until next period. Which assertion relates directly to the income statement in the year under audit being overstated for sales?
    I. Existence
    II. Occurrence
    (A) I only
    (B) II only
    (C) Both I and II
    (D) Neither I nor II

250. The reporting company records sales revenue and accounts receivable near the end of the year because a sales order has been received. However, the earnings process will not be complete until next period. Which assertion is affected in the current year?
    I. Occurrence
    II. Existence
    (A) I only
    (B) II only
    (C) Both I and II
    (D) Neither I nor II

251. Phillip is the auditor for the Andrinua Corp. A building is recorded by Andrinua Corp. for $750,000, which is the correct cost, but the building actually belongs to another company, Desimone Inc., and is only being used by Andrinua Corp. through an operating lease. Which assertion is impacted?
    I. Rights and obligations
    II. Completeness

    (A) I only
    (B) II only
    (C) Both I and II
    (D) Neither I nor II

252. Which of the following is an assertion found under the category of presentation and disclosure?
    I. Completeness
    II. Classification and understandability

    (A) I only
    (B) II only
    (C) Both I and II
    (D) Neither I nor II

253. Which of the following is an assertion found in all three categories of assertions?
    I. Completeness
    II. Rights and obligations

    (A) I only
    (B) II only
    (C) Both I and II
    (D) Neither I nor II

254. An asset is categorized as a fixed asset when it should have been recorded as inventory. Which assertion is affected?
    I. Rights and obligations
    II. Classification

    (A) I only
    (B) II only
    (C) Both I and II
    (D) Neither I nor II

255. Which of the following is NOT an assertion category?
    I. Presentation and disclosure
    II. Classes of transactions and events
    III. Completeness

    (A) I and II only
    (B) II and III only
    (C) III only
    (D) II only

CHAPTER 10

Evidence Gathering and Transaction Cycles, Part 1

256. When an independent auditor uses professional judgment to make decisions about the "nature, extent, and timing" of audit procedures, what does the term *nature* refer to?
   I. The amount of testing to be performed
  II. The type of test to be performed

(A) I only
(B) II only
(C) Both I and II
(D) Neither I nor II

257. Which of the following involves a theft of receivables followed by a delay in the posting of credits to specific customer accounts?
   I. Kiting
  II. Lapping

(A) I only
(B) II only
(C) Both I and II
(D) Neither I nor II

258. Corey is the auditor for Arthur Inc. When a customer pays Arthur Inc. by check and mails the check to Arthur Inc., Carol, the secretary, gathers the customer checks from their envelopes. For good internal control, what should Carol NOT have the authority to do?
   I. Deposit the customer checks into Arthur Inc.'s bank account
  II. Prepare a listing of the checks received
  III. Post the credits to the individual customer's accounts

(A) I and III only
(B) III only
(C) I, II, and III
(D) II and III only

259. In a revenue cycle, which of the following departments prepares the sales order and approves the customer for credit?

	Preparation of Sales Order	Authorization of Credit
(A)	Credit department	Credit department
(B)	Credit department	Sales department
(C)	Sales department	Credit department
(D)	Sales department	Sales department

260. Prior to shipping, a copy of the sales order is:

    I. Sent to the billings department to verify that the shipment is going to an approved customer who is not over any credit limit

    II. Sent to the billings department to enable the billings department to prepare a bill of lading

(A) I only
(B) II only
(C) Both I and II
(D) Neither I nor II

261. In a revenue cycle, a copy of the approved sales order is sent to which department(s)?

    I. Billings

    II. Shipping

(A) I only
(B) II only
(C) Both I and II
(D) Neither I nor II

262. The billings department prepares the sales invoice after receiving a copy of which of the following documents?

    I. Purchase requisition

    II. Sales order

    III. Bill of lading

(A) II only
(B) II and III only
(C) I, II, and III
(D) III only

263. Within the revenue cycle, which of the following departments maintains a pending or open file but takes no action until a copy of both the sales order and the bill of lading are received?

(A) Sales department
(B) Billings department
(C) Credit department
(D) Warehouse department

264. In the revenue cycle, which of the following departments matches the information on the sales order and bill of lading and verifies that each is properly authorized?

(A) Credit department
(B) Sales department
(C) Warehouse department
(D) Billings department

265. Within a proper segregation of duties for the revenue cycle, which of the following departments represents an example of custody?

(A) Shipping department
(B) Billings department
(C) Receiving room
(D) Warehouse department

266. Within the revenue and purchasing cycle of an organization, which of the following departments normally has the authority to move goods only within the organization?

I. Warehouse
II. Shipping department
III. Receiving room

(A) I and II only
(B) III only
(C) I only
(D) I and III only

267. Within a proper segregation of duties for the revenue cycle, which of the following departments serves an authorization function?

(A) Credit department
(B) Billings department
(C) Purchasing department
(D) Shipping department

268. Within the revenue cycle, for proper segregation of duties, which of the following departments normally prepares the bill of lading and the sales invoice?

Bill of Lading	Sales Invoice
(A) Billings department	Sales department
(B) Billings department	Shipping department
(C) Shipping department	Sales department
(D) Shipping department	Billings department

269. For proper segregation of duties in the revenue cycle, the warehouse department delivers merchandise to the shipping department. Before accepting the goods, the shipping department should:
  I. Inspect the goods for damage
  II. Count the items and compare the number and other information to the sales order

(A) I only
(B) II only
(C) Both I and II
(D) Neither I nor II

270. For proper segregation of duties in a revenue cycle, the shipping department:
  I. Prepares the bill of lading and sends a copy to inventory accounting to update the perpetual records
  II. Sends a copy of the bill of lading to the billings department

(A) I only
(B) II only
(C) Both I and II
(D) Neither I nor II

271. In what order are these three forms usually generated in a credit sales system: bill of lading, sales invoice, sales order?

(A) Sales order, bill of lading, sales invoice
(B) Sales order, sales invoice, bill of lading
(C) Sales invoice, sales order, bill of lading
(D) Bill of lading, sales order, sales invoice

272. In a revenue cycle, which of the following departments does NOT prepare the sales order, the sales invoice, or the bill of lading?

(A) Sales department
(B) Warehouse department
(C) Shipping department
(D) Billings department

273. Shann, CPA, is performing an audit of Cove Corp., a wholesaler of consumer products. Shann begins with entries in the sales journal and makes sure that there is a sales invoice to support it.
   I. This is a test of the existence/occurrence assertion.
   II. Shann is probably concerned with overstatement of revenue.

   (A) I only
   (B) II only
   (C) Both I and II
   (D) Neither I nor II

274. An auditor begins with a sample of bills of lading and traces forward into the accounting records. Which of the following is correct?
   I. The auditor is testing the completeness assertion for sales.
   II. If there is no sales invoice found for a particular bill of lading, the auditor fears that sales may be overstated.

   (A) I only
   (B) II only
   (C) Both I and II
   (D) Neither I nor II

275. An auditor begins with a sample of bills of lading and traces forward into the accounting records. If a sales invoice was not found for a particular shipment, the auditor could suspect that goods were shipped out:
   I. Fraudulently
   II. On consignment

   (A) I only
   (B) II only
   (C) Both I and II
   (D) Neither I nor II

276. An auditor is concerned that the company is increasing reported net income by producing sales invoices for goods that were never ordered or shipped.
   I. The auditor should select a sample of sales invoices and verify that matching sales orders and bills of lading exist.
   II. If the auditor finds sales invoices with no related shipping documents, this would be a test of the occurrence assertion rather than the completeness assertion.

   (A) I only
   (B) II only
   (C) Both I and II
   (D) Neither I nor II

277. An auditor is concerned that sales are being made and shipped but are never billed or recorded. The auditor believes that employees may be stealing company assets in this way.
  I. The auditor should select a sample of bills of lading and verify that sales invoices do exist.
  II. Shipments on consignment would not explain the missing sales invoices.

(A) I only
(B) II only
(C) Both I and II
(D) Neither I nor II

278. Tracing shipping documents to prenumbered sales invoices:
  I. Provides evidence that shipments to customers were properly invoiced
  II. Is a test for overstatement of sales rather than understatement

(A) I only
(B) II only
(C) Both I and II
(D) Neither I nor II

279. If an auditor starts with the entries in the sales journal and seeks supporting documentation to corroborate:
  I. The auditor is testing the completeness assertion
  II. The auditor would be looking for sales orders rather than shipping documents

(A) I only
(B) II only
(C) Both I and II
(D) Neither I nor II

280. If the objective of an auditor's test of details is to detect a possible understatement of sales, the auditor most likely would trace transactions from the:

(A) Sales invoices to the shipping documents
(B) Cash receipts journal to the sales journal
(C) Shipping documents to the sales invoices
(D) Sales journal to the cash receipts journal

281. Which of the following is a substantive test for accounts receivable in the subsequent period?
    I. Examining how much bad debt was written off shortly after year-end
    II. Examining how much cash was actually collected shortly after year-end

    (A) I only
    (B) II only
    (C) Both I and II
    (D) Neither I nor II

282. Which of the following substantive procedures provides evidence of the existence assertion for accounts receivable in the subsequent period?
    I. Examining how much bad debt was written off shortly after year-end
    II. Examining how much cash was actually collected shortly after year-end

    (A) I only
    (B) II only
    (C) Both I and II
    (D) Neither I nor II

283. Which assertion is being most directly addressed when an auditor selects a sample of sales invoices and compares it to the subsequent journal entries recorded in the sales journal?

    (A) Occurrence
    (B) Classification
    (C) Accuracy
    (D) Completeness

284. When an auditor gathers evidence within a revenue cycle, tracing sales invoices to the client's revenue account provides evidence that:
    I. Approved spending limits are not exceeded
    II. Sales are not understated

    (A) I only
    (B) II only
    (C) Both I and II
    (D) Neither I nor II

285. An auditor plans to confirm a sample of accounts receivable. An auditor confirms receivables primarily to obtain evidence about:
  I. The valuation assertion
  II. The existence assertion

(A) I only
(B) II only
(C) Both I and II
(D) Neither I nor II

286. To test the existence assertion for accounts receivable an auditor would:
  I. Send accounts receivable confirmation requests to a sample of client customers
  II. Inspect and verify the credit-granting policies of the client

(A) I only
(B) II only
(C) Both I and II
(D) Neither I nor II

287. An auditor is confirming receivables and was planning to use negative confirmations. The auditor assessed inherent risk and control risk and found them to be higher than anticipated.
  I. The auditor should consider switching from negative confirmations to positive confirmations.
  II. Positive confirmations are more likely to be used when the acceptable level of detection risk is especially low.

(A) I only
(B) II only
(C) Both I and II
(D) Neither I nor II

288. For good internal controls in a revenue cycle, which of the following correctly describes the credit manager's duties?
  I. Should report directly to the vice president of sales
  II. Should authorize a write-off of an uncollectible account

(A) I only
(B) II only
(C) Both I and II
(D) Neither I nor II

289. An auditor must know the relationship between inventory errors and the effect on net income. If a client's ending inventory is overstated:

    I. Net income is overstated because gross profit is overstated

    II. Cost of goods sold is understated

(A) I only

(B) II only

(C) Both I and II

(D) Neither I nor II

290. When an auditor examines a client's inventory, items shipped out on consignment by the client:

    I. Belong to the client rather than the consignee

    II. Are a concern to the auditor because of the rights and obligations assertion

(A) I only

(B) II only

(C) Both I and II

(D) Neither I nor II

291. In a purchasing cycle, the receiving room gets a copy of the:

    I. Purchase requisition

    II. Purchase order

(A) I only

(B) II only

(C) Both I and II

(D) Neither I nor II

292. How many different documents are generally involved in the purchasing cycle?

(A) 5

(B) 4

(C) 3

(D) 2

293. Put these documents in the order in which they appear in a purchasing cycle:

    I. Purchase order

    II. Receiving report

    III. Purchase invoice

    IV. Purchase requisition

(A) IV, I, II, III

(B) IV, II, III, I

(C) I, II, III, IV

(D) I, II, IV, III

294. In a purchasing cycle, which of the following departments reconciles the purchase order and receiving report and approves the purchase invoice for payment?

(A) Purchasing department
(B) Billings department
(C) Receiving room
(D) Accounts payable

295. In the purchasing cycle, which of the following departments does NOT receive a copy of the receiving report?

  I. Accounts payable
 II. The department that prepared the purchase requisition

(A) I only
(B) II only
(C) Both I and II
(D) Neither I nor II

296. Which of the following documents is NOT prepared by the purchasing department?

   I. Purchase order
  II. Purchase invoice
III. Purchase requisition

(A) I and III only
(B) I and II only
(C) II and III only
(D) III only

297. Which of the following documents is prepared outside the organization?

   I. Purchase invoice
  II. Receiving report
III. Voucher package

(A) I and III only
(B) I only
(C) III only
(D) I and II only

298. For effective internal control purposes, the vouchers payable department generally should:

   I. Establish the agreement of the vendor's invoice with the receiving report and purchase order

  II. Deliberately remove the quantity ordered on the receiving department copy of the purchase order

(A) I only
(B) II only
(C) Both I and II
(D) Neither I nor II

299. Within a client's purchasing cycle there are various departments. Which of the following departments approves the voucher for payment and which department pays the vendor?

	Approves the Voucher	Pays the Vendor
(A)	Accounts payable	Accounts payable
(B)	Accounts payable	Cash receipts
(C)	Accounts payable	Cash disbursements
(D)	Cash disbursements	Cash disbursements

300. In a purchasing cycle that uses a voucher system, which of the following forms is attached to the voucher and becomes part of the voucher package?

   I. Purchase order
  II. Receiving report
 III. Bill of lading

(A) I and II only
(B) I only
(C) I, II, and III
(D) II only

301. In the purchasing cycle, which of the following is correct regarding the voucher and the voucher package?

   I. The voucher is the document that acknowledges the liability and approves payment.

  II. The backup documentation (a copy of all four forms) is attached in what is called a voucher package.

 III. The voucher package is recorded in the voucher register and forwarded to cash disbursements for payment.

(A) I and II only
(B) II and III only
(C) I and III only
(D) I, II, and III

302. In a purchasing cycle that uses a voucher system, good internal control dictates that which of the following departments should be responsible for signing the check and mailing the check to the vendor?

	Signs the Check	Mails the Check to the Vendor
(A)	Cash disbursements	Vouchers payable
(B)	Vouchers payable	Cash disbursements
(C)	Cash disbursements	Cash disbursements
(D)	Vouchers payable	Vouchers payable

303. In a cash disbursements cycle that employs a voucher system, which of the following departments cancels or perforates the voucher package so that the voucher cannot be paid more than once and then mails the check to the vendor?

(A) Cash disbursements
(B) Vouchers payable
(C) Purchasing
(D) Receiving

304. In an audit, in the evidence-gathering stage of the purchasing cycle, the auditor would examine a sample of paid vouchers to gather evidence as to whether each voucher is:

I. Supported by a vendor invoice
II. Stamped "paid" by the check signer

(A) I only
(B) II only
(C) Both I and II
(D) Neither I nor II

305. To provide assurance that each voucher is submitted and paid only once, an auditor would examine a sample of paid vouchers and determine whether each voucher is:

I. Supported by a vendor invoice and purchase order
II. Stamped "paid" by the check signer

(A) I only
(B) II only
(C) Both I and II
(D) Neither I nor II

306. An auditor vouches a sample of entries in the voucher register to the supporting documents. Which assertion would this test most likely support?
  I. Existence or occurrence
  II. Completeness

  (A) I only
  (B) II only
  (C) Both I and II
  (D) Neither I nor II

307. In a properly designed internal control system, which department would match vendors' invoices with receiving reports and also recompute the calculations on vendors' invoices?
  I. Purchasing department
  II. Vouchers payable
  III. Cash disbursements

  (A) I and II only
  (B) II and III only
  (C) I and III only
  (D) II only

308. Which of the following documents is part of a purchasing cycle?
  I. Receiving report
  II. Bill of lading

  (A) I only
  (B) II only
  (C) Both I and II
  (D) Neither I nor II

309. If the auditor is testing the completeness assertion for accounts payable, a sample of which of the following documents would the auditor likely begin with?
  I. Purchase invoices
  II. Receiving reports

  (A) I only
  (B) II only
  (C) Both I and II
  (D) Neither I nor II

310. An auditor traced a sample of purchase orders and the related receiving reports to the purchases journal and the cash disbursements journal. The purpose of this substantive audit procedure most likely was to:
  I. Determine that purchases were properly recorded
  II. Test the existence or occurrence assertion for accounts payable

(A) I only
(B) II only
(C) Both I and II
(D) Neither I nor II

311. In the purchasing cycle, when the auditor is testing an existence or occurrence assertion, the auditor:
  I. Starts with the supporting documents and looks to see if the transaction was in fact recorded
  II. Starts with the recorded balances and works backward seeking support

(A) I only
(B) II only
(C) Both I and II
(D) Neither I nor II

312. Which of the following is an example of audit evidence generated by the client in the purchasing cycle?
  I. Bills of lading
  II. Receiving reports

(A) I only
(B) II only
(C) Both I and II
(D) Neither I nor II

313. Which of the following documents are examples of audit evidence generated by the client?
  I. Vendor invoices and packing slips
  II. Bills of lading and accounts receivable confirmations

(A) I only
(B) II only
(C) Both I and II
(D) Neither I nor II

314. An auditor selects transactions recorded in the voucher register for three days prior to the end of the fiscal year and compares each of these entries to the related receiving report and purchase invoice. Which of those two documents should indicate the FOB point when title changed hands, and which document should indicate the date the goods were received?

	Title Changed Hands	Receipt of the Goods
(A)	Purchase invoice	Purchase invoice
(B)	Purchase invoice	Receiving report
(C)	Receiving report	Purchase invoice
(D)	Receiving report	Receiving report

315. Which of the following procedures would an auditor most likely perform in searching for unrecorded liabilities?
  - I. Trace a sample of accounts payable entries recorded just before year-end to the unmatched receiving report file
  - II. Trace a sample of cash disbursements recorded just after year-end to receiving reports and vendor invoices

  (A) I only
  (B) II only
  (C) Both I and II
  (D) Neither I nor II

316. Observation of physical inventory counts provides evidence about which of the following assertions?
  - I. Existence
  - II. Completeness

  (A) I only
  (B) II only
  (C) Both I and II
  (D) Neither I nor II

317. As part of the process of observing a client's physical inventories, an auditor would be able to determine:
  - I. Any change in the method of pricing from prior years
  - II. The existence of outstanding purchase commitments

  (A) I only
  (B) II only
  (C) Both I and II
  (D) Neither I nor II

318. With regard to inventory, the rights and obligations assertion might be tested by the auditor:

    I. Inspecting consignment agreements and contracts

    II. Confirming inventory held at outside locations

(A) I only

(B) II only

(C) Both I and II

(D) Neither I nor II

319. An auditor's observation procedures with respect to well-kept perpetual inventories that are periodically checked by physical counts may be performed at which of the following times?

(A) Before the end of the year

(B) At year-end

(C) After year-end

(D) All of the above

320. Which of the following are the most efficient and effective means of gathering evidence regarding a client's inventory held at a public warehouse?

	Most Efficient	**Most Effective**
(A)	Observation	Observation
(B)	Confirmation	Confirmation
(C)	Confirmation	Observation
(D)	Observation	Confirmation

321. Fritz is an auditor for Barbarino Corp., a manufacturing entity. Which of the following procedures would Fritz likely perform to determine whether slow-moving, defective, and obsolete items included in inventory are properly identified?

    I. Tour the manufacturing plant or production facility

    II. Compare inventory balances to anticipated sales volume

(A) I only

(B) II only

(C) Both I and II

(D) Neither I nor II

322. When observing inventory, which of the following is a purpose for the auditor taking test counts of the client's inventory?

    I. To help ensure the accuracy of the client unit count

    II. To aid later verification of final cost figures

(A) I only

(B) II only

(C) Both I and II

(D) Neither I nor II

323. The auditor should test the client's physical inventory report by tracing test counts taken by the auditor to the client's physical inventory count. Which assertion is affected by this test?

(A) Completeness
(B) Existence
(C) Rights and obligations
(D) Valuation

324. When gathering evidence regarding inventory, the auditor would begin with the client's physical inventory listing and compare to the auditor's test count. Which assertion would be tested by this procedure?

(A) Rights and obligations
(B) Existence
(C) Completeness
(D) Classification and understandability

325. When an auditor starts with the tags and compares the tags to the detailed inventory listings, he or she is testing for:

I. Existence
II. Completeness

(A) I only
(B) II only
(C) Both I and II
(D) Neither I nor II

326. Tracing from inventory tags to the inventory listing schedule verifies the:

I. Completeness of the schedule
II. Existence of the items

(A) I only
(B) II only
(C) Both I and II
(D) Neither I nor II

327. Tracing from the inventory schedule to the inventory tags verifies the:

I. Validity (existence) of the items
II. Completeness of the inventory schedule

(A) I only
(B) II only
(C) Both I and II
(D) Neither I nor II

328. Tracing from receiving reports and vendors' invoices to the perpetual inventory listing are procedures used to verify:
   I. Completeness of the inventory listing
   II. Existence of the inventory

(A) I only
(B) II only
(C) Both I and II
(D) Neither I nor II

329. The Lexy Corporation buys and sells handbags. In Year 1, the average number of days that it took to sell a handbag was 14. In Year 2, because of the downturn in the economy, the average number of days that it took to sell a handbag rose to 25.

Which of management's assertions about the balance being reported as inventory on the company's balance sheet would be of most concern to the independent auditor?

(A) Presentation
(B) Valuation
(C) Existence
(D) Completeness

330. Alan is performing an audit of Berman Industries Inc. During the evidence-gathering phase for inventory, Alan would verify that certain inventory, owned by Berman Industries at year-end, is included in the count. Which of the following should be included in the year-end count?
   I. Inventory purchased FOB shipping point and still in transit at year-end
   II. Inventory shipped out on consignment by Berman Industries on December 31

(A) I only
(B) II only
(C) Both I and II
(D) Neither I nor II

331. When auditing inventories, an auditor would least likely verify that:
(A) The financial statement presentation of inventories is appropriate
(B) Damaged goods and obsolete items have been properly accounted for
(C) All inventory owned by the client is on hand at the time of the count
(D) The client has used proper inventory pricing

332. Brunner is doing an audit of Tucker Corp. Tests designed to detect purchases made by Tucker before the end of the year that have been recorded in the subsequent year most likely would provide assurance about Tucker's assertion regarding:
   I. Rights and obligations
   II. Cutoff

(A) I only
(B) II only
(C) Both I and II
(D) Neither I nor II

333. Alex Corp. is a manufacturer. Under the category of presentation and disclosure, completeness is an assertion that relates to inventory disclosure. Which of the following inventory balances would Alex Corp. NOT be required to disclose?
   I. Work in process
   II. Raw materials

(A) I only
(B) II only
(C) Both I and II
(D) Neither I nor II

334. With regard to inventory, assertions about accuracy relate to:
   I. Whether data related to recorded transactions have been included in the financial statements at appropriate amounts
   II. Cutoff testing for purchases

(A) I only
(B) II only
(C) Both I and II
(D) Neither I nor II

335. Inventories should be reduced, when appropriate, to replacement cost or net realizable value, to support management's assertion of:
   I. Valuation
   II. Understandability
   III. Existence

(A) I and III only
(B) I only
(C) I and II only
(D) I, II, and III

336. Su is performing an audit of Allegra Corp. With regard to assertions relating to inventory, understandability and classification might be tested by:
  I. Confirming inventories pledged under loan agreements
  II. Examining drafts of the financial statements for appropriate balance sheet classification

(A) I only
(B) II only
(C) Both I and II
(D) Neither I nor II

CHAPTER 11

Audit Sampling

337. When using statistical sampling to estimate a rate (sampling for attributes):
   I. The auditor is frequently assessing control risk
   II. The auditor is concerned with overstatement of an account balance

   (A) I only
   (B) II only
   (C) Both I and II
   (D) Neither I nor II

338. In statistical sampling, which of the following factors regarding the population is considered in determining the sample size for a test of controls?
   I. Expected error or deviation rate
   II. Tolerable error or deviation rate

   (A) I only
   (B) II only
   (C) Both I and II
   (D) Neither I nor II

339. An auditor is sampling for attributes, that is, testing controls. Which of the following is correct regarding sample size when the auditor determines that the expected error rate is different from that originally expected?

   (A) If the expected error rate has risen, the sample size will be reduced.
   (B) If the expected error rate has fallen, the sample size will be increased.
   (C) If the expected error rate has risen, the sample size will be increased.
   (D) Both A and B

340. An auditor is estimating an error rate for a test of controls. The auditor must set a level of sampling risk that is viewed as acceptable. For some reason, the auditor decides to reduce the allowable level of sampling risk for a particular test. Which of the following statements is correct?

    I. The auditor will likely select a smaller sample than originally anticipated.

    II. If the auditor increases sample size, the chance that the sample will have characteristics different from the population goes down.

(A) I only

(B) II only

(C) Both I and II

(D) Neither I nor II

341. Wes is performing an audit of Turner Corp. Wes has identified a control activity that will reduce the assessment of control risk if it is operating effectively and efficiently. Wes has decided to perform sampling for attributes. Wes believes the actual error rate of this activity is 2 percent but can tolerate an error rate of up to 5 percent and still feel that the control is reliable. Wes wants to reduce sampling risk to a 10 percent level and be 90 percent sure that the sample is representative of the population. Which of the following statements is correct?

    I. If Wes were suddenly to change his assessment of the actual error from 2 percent to 3 percent, the sample size would have to be increased.

    II. If Wes wants to reduce the allowable level of risk from 10 percent to 5 percent, the sample size will have to be increased.

(A) I only

(B) II only

(C) Both I and II

(D) Neither I nor II

342. An auditor has identified a control activity that will reduce the assessment of control risk if it is operating effectively and efficiently. The auditor has decided to perform sampling for attributes. The auditor believes the actual error rate of this activity is 2 percent but can tolerate a rate of up to 5 percent. The auditor wants to reduce sampling risk to 10 percent. The appropriate sample size is determined and selected, and an error rate of 3 percent is discovered. A chart is examined that indicates that the upper deviation rate is 6.4 percent. Which of the following statements is correct?

    I. The allowance for sampling risk is 3.4 percent.

    II. The auditor should determine that the control is working effectively and reduce control risk, since the sample rate of 3 percent is below the tolerable rate of 5 percent.

(A) I only

(B) II only

(C) Both I and II

(D) Neither I nor II

343. The auditor believes the actual error rate of an activity is 2 percent but can tolerate a rate of up to 5 percent. The auditor wants to reduce sampling risk to 10 percent. The appropriate sample size is determined and selected, and an error rate of 3 percent is discovered. A chart is examined that indicates that the upper deviation rate is 4.4 percent. Which is correct?
  I. The auditor should assess the control activity as having too many errors.
  II. The tolerable rate is higher than the upper deviation rate.

(A) I only
(B) II only
(C) Both I and II
(D) Neither I nor II

344. The sample rate of deviation plus the allowance for sampling risk is equal to the:
  I. Upper deviation rate
  II. Tolerable deviation rate

(A) I only
(B) II only
(C) Both I and II
(D) Neither I nor II

345. The likelihood of assessing control risk too high relates to the:
  I. Effectiveness of the audit
  II. Efficiency of the audit

(A) I only
(B) II only
(C) Both I and II
(D) Neither I nor II

346. When an auditor is estimating an account balance, the auditor must set a level of sampling risk that is viewed as acceptable. For some reason, the auditor decides to reduce the allowable level of sampling risk for a particular test. Which of the following is correct?
  I. The auditor will have to select a larger sample than originally anticipated.
  II. This type of sampling is known as sampling for variables.

(A) I only
(B) II only
(C) Both I and II
(D) Neither I nor II

347. Which of the following illustrates the concept of sampling risk?
   I. A randomly chosen sample may not be representative of the population as a whole on the characteristic of interest.
   II. An auditor may select audit procedures that are not appropriate to achieve the specific objective.
   (A) I only
   (B) II only
   (C) Both I and II
   (D) Neither I nor II

348. When an auditor is estimating an account balance:
   I. The auditor must set a limit for the largest amount of discovered problem that can be tolerated before the account balance is considered not fairly presented.
   II. As the amount of misstatement that an auditor can tolerate rises, the appropriate sample size will have to go up.
   (A) I only
   (B) II only
   (C) Both I and II
   (D) Neither I nor II

349. In performing attribute sampling, which of the following would have a significant effect on the sample size?
   I. Number of items in the population
   II. Tolerable deviation rate
   (A) I only
   (B) II only
   (C) Both I and II
   (D) Neither I nor II

350. In performing variable sampling, which of the following would have a significant effect on the sample size?
   I. Number of items in the population
   II. Allowable level of risk
   (A) I only
   (B) II only
   (C) Both I and II
   (D) Neither I nor II

351. While performing a test of details during an audit, an auditor determined that the sample results supported the conclusion that the recorded account balance was materially misstated. It was, in fact, not materially misstated. This situation illustrates the risk of:

(A) Assessing control risk too high
(B) Assessing control risk too low
(C) Incorrect rejection
(D) Incorrect acceptance

352. While performing a test of details during an audit, an auditor determined that the sample results supported the conclusion that the recorded account balance was fairly presented in accordance with GAAP. It was, in fact, materially misstated. This situation illustrates the risk of:

(A) Assessing control risk too high
(B) Assessing control risk too low
(C) Incorrect rejection
(D) Incorrect acceptance

353. The expected balance of a client's accounts receivable is being estimated by the auditor. The expected rate of error in the account balance is 3 percent. The auditor has established a tolerable rate of 5 percent. The auditor would probably NOT use:

(A) Stratified sampling
(B) Variable sampling
(C) PPS sampling
(D) Attribute sampling

354. A primary feature of using generalized audit software packages to audit the financial statements of a client that uses a computerized system is that the auditor:

I. May access information stored on computer files while having a limited understanding of the client's hardware and software features
II. Is able to sample and test a much higher percentage of transactions

(A) I only
(B) II only
(C) Both I and II
(D) Neither I nor II

CHAPTER 12

Evidence Gathering and Transaction Cycles, Part 2

355. Which of the following is correct regarding the auditor's use of the standard bank confirmation?
   I. The usefulness of the standard bank confirmation request may be limited because the bank employee who completes the form may be unaware of all the financial relationships that the bank has with the client.
   II. The standard bank confirmation should request balances of all bank accounts, except for accounts that were closed during the year.

(A) I only
(B) II only
(C) Both I and II
(D) Neither I nor II

356. When auditing a client's year-end cash balance, which of the following is an auditor-prepared document specifically designed to detect kiting?
   I. Bank reconciliation
   II. Bank cutoff statement
   III. Bank transfer schedule

(A) I, II, and III
(B) II and III only
(C) III only
(D) I and III only

357. The auditor should obtain bank cutoff statements that include transactions for 10 to 15 days after year-end. The information on the bank cutoff statements should agree with:
   I. The outstanding checks at year-end on the bank reconciliation
   II. The deposits in transit at year-end on the bank reconciliation

(A) I only
(B) II only
(C) Both I and II
(D) Neither I nor II

358. When auditing cash, client checks dated after year-end would NOT be included in the:
  I. Bank cutoff statement
  II. Year-end outstanding check list
(A) I only
(B) II only
(C) Both I and II
(D) Neither I nor II

359. Which of the following is correct?
  I. A bank cutoff statement is used to verify the items appearing on a bank reconciliation.
  II. If a deposit in transit from the bank reconciliation is not recorded by the bank in a reasonable period of time, the auditor should be suspicious that the deposit was not really in transit.
(A) I only
(B) II only
(C) Both I and II
(D) Neither I nor II

360. Regarding reliability of audit evidence, municipal property tax bills prepared in the client's name are an example of:
(A) Internal evidence
(B) External evidence
(C) Evidence that is less reliable than internal evidence
(D) Evidence that is more reliable than external evidence

361. Koko, CPA, is preparing an internal control questionnaire regarding equipment purchases during an audit of Conisha Corp. Which of the following questions would Koko likely include on an internal control questionnaire concerning the initiation and execution of equipment transactions?
  I. Are prenumbered purchase orders used for equipment and periodically accounted for?
  II. Are requests for purchases of equipment reviewed for consideration of soliciting competitive bids?
(A) I only
(B) II only
(C) Both I and II
(D) Neither I nor II

362. Which of the following explanations most likely would satisfy an auditor who questions management about significant debits to the accumulated depreciation accounts?
  I. The prior year's depreciation expense was erroneously understated.
  II. Plant assets were retired during the year.

(A) I only
(B) II only
(C) Both I and II
(D) Neither I nor II

363. Determining that proper amounts of depreciation are expensed provides assurance about management's assertion of:
  I. Valuation, allocation, and accuracy
  II. Existence

(A) I only
(B) II only
(C) Both I and II
(D) Neither I nor II

364. Testing to see whether equipment listed in the accounting records is physically present in the plant and still in service is an effective way to:
  I. Test whether unrecorded disposals of equipment have occurred
  II. Test whether depreciation was taken on each item of equipment during the year

(A) I only
(B) II only
(C) Both I and II
(D) Neither I nor II

365. When auditing property, plant, and equipment, which of the following would an auditor do to search for unrecorded additions?
  I. Examine the repairs and maintenance account
  II. Select certain items of equipment from the accounting records and locate them in the plant

(A) I only
(B) II only
(C) Both I and II
(D) Neither I nor II

366. An analysis of which of the following accounts would NOT aid in verifying that all fixed assets have been capitalized?
  I. Repair and maintenance
  II. Depreciation expense

(A) I only
(B) II only
(C) Both I and II
(D) Neither I nor II

367. When auditing equipment, an auditor would examine insurance records and tour the client's facility to:
  I. Search for unrecorded disposals of assets
  II. Search for assets that were erroneously charged to expense

(A) I only
(B) II only
(C) Both I and II
(D) Neither I nor II

368. Analyzing the repairs and maintenance account provides evidence that:
  I. Obsolete plant and equipment assets were written off before year-end
  II. All recorded plant and equipment assets actually exist

(A) I only
(B) II only
(C) Both I and II
(D) Neither I nor II

369. An auditor who determines that proper amounts of depreciation are expensed provides assurance about management's assertion of:
  I. Completeness
  II. Rights and obligations

(A) I only
(B) II only
(C) Both I and II
(D) Neither I nor II

370. In testing for unrecorded retirements of equipment, an auditor most likely would:

    I. Select items of equipment from the accounting records and then locate them during the plant tour

    II. Scan the general journal for unusual equipment additions and excessive debits to repairs and maintenance expense

(A) I only

(B) II only

(C) Both I and II

(D) Neither I nor II

371. An auditor would expect to find significant debits to the accumulated depreciation account if, during the year, assets were:

    I. Sold

    II. Retired

    III. Permanently impaired

(A) I, II, and III

(B) I and II only

(C) I and III only

(D) II and III only

372. Which is correct when testing notes payable or other long-term liabilities?

    I. An auditor should review the minutes of the meetings of the board of directors.

    II. A bank cutoff statement is reviewed as part of the auditor's search for unrecorded long-term liabilities.

(A) I only

(B) II only

(C) Both I and II

(D) Neither I nor II

373. When an auditor is searching for unrecorded liabilities, which assertion is directly impacted?

    I. Valuation

    II. Completeness

    III. Existence

(A) I only

(B) I and II only

(C) II only

(D) I, II, and III

374. The auditor will read which of the following to gather evidence regarding contingencies?
    I.   The minutes of the board of directors meetings
    II. The management rep letter
    III. Letters from client's legal counsel

    (A) I and II only
    (B) II and III only
    (C) I and III only
    (D) I, II, and III

375. The auditor will read which of the following to gather evidence regarding contingencies?
    I.   Client contracts that contain a liquidated damages clause
    II. Client loan agreements that contain debt covenants

    (A) I only
    (B) II only
    (C) Both I and II
    (D) Neither I nor II

376. With regard to contingent losses, some method has to be derived to corroborate the company's assessment of:
    I.   The likelihood of each loss
    II. The estimated amount of each loss

    (A) I only
    (B) II only
    (C) Both I and II
    (D) Neither I nor II

377. Which of the following is considered a procedure involving the auditor's search for contingent liabilities?
    I.   Reviewing a bank confirmation letter
    II. Reviewing a customer's response to a negative confirmation
    III. Examining client invoices received from professionals who have provided service

    (A) I only
    (B) I and III only
    (C) I, II, and III
    (D) III only

378. Information about unasserted claims should come to the auditor from the:
    I. Client's attorney
    II. Client
    (A) I only
    (B) II only
    (C) Both I and II
    (D) Neither I nor II

379. The primary source of information to be reported about litigation, claims, and assessments is the:
    (A) Client's lawyer
    (B) Court records
    (C) Client's management
    (D) Independent auditor

380. A lawyer's response to an auditor's inquiry concerning litigation, claims, and assessments may be limited to matters that are considered individually or collectively material to the client's financial statements. Which parties should reach an understanding on the limits of materiality for this purpose?
    (A) The auditor and the client's management
    (B) The client's audit committee and the lawyer
    (C) The client's management and the lawyer
    (D) The lawyer and the auditor

381. Which of the following procedures would accomplish the audit objective of searching for unrecorded long-term liabilities?
    I. Examining unusual and large cash receipts, especially near the end of the year
    II. Reconciling interest expense to the amount of long-term debt reported at year-end
    (A) I only
    (B) II only
    (C) Both I and II
    (D) Neither I nor II

382. An auditor must perform analytical procedures in the:
    I. Planning stage of an audit
    II. Internal control stage of an audit
    (A) I only
    (B) II only
    (C) Both I and II
    (D) Neither I nor II

383. Analytical procedures are required in which stage of the audit?
   I. Evidence-gathering stage
   II. Overall review stage

(A) I only
(B) II only
(C) Both I and II
(D) Neither I nor II

384. Which of the following payroll control activities would most effectively ensure that payment is made only for work performed?
   I. Require all employees to record arrival and departure by using the time clock.
   II. Require all employees to have their direct supervisors approve their time cards.

(A) I only
(B) II only
(C) Both I and II
(D) Neither I nor II

385. Segregation of duties between human resources and payroll departments is an important control to ensure that:
   I. Only valid employees receive paychecks
   II. All payroll checks are printed unsigned

(A) I only
(B) II only
(C) Both I and II
(D) Neither I nor II

386. Which of the following activities performed by a department supervisor would be considered an incompatible function?
   I.   Distributing paychecks directly to department employees
   II. Approving a summary of hours each employee worked during the pay period
   III. Setting the pay rate for departmental employees

(A) I and II only
(B) I and III only
(C) II and III only
(D) II only

387. The occurrence assertion as it relates to payroll transactions would correspond to which of the following audit objectives?

    I. To determine that all payroll checks were issued to valid employees for hours actually worked

    II. To determine if any payroll checks were missing

(A) I only

(B) II only

(C) Both I and II

(D) Neither I nor II

388. An auditor recomputes payroll deductions and verifies the preparation of the monthly payroll account bank reconciliation to provide evidence for which of the following assertions?

(A) Existence

(B) Completeness

(C) Accuracy

(D) Cutoff

389. Which of the following circumstances most likely would cause an auditor to assess control risk at a high level for payroll?

    I. Payroll checks generally are disbursed by the same person (or the same department) each payday.

    II. Employee time cards are approved by individual departmental supervisors.

(A) I only

(B) II only

(C) Both I and II

(D) Neither I nor II

390. The independent auditor makes an evaluation of the internal audit staff as a procedure in the assessment of control risk. Normally, the independent auditor will look at the internal auditor's:

    I. Competency

    II. Objectivity

(A) I only

(B) II only

(C) Both I and II

(D) Neither I nor II

391. In assessing the competence of internal auditors, an independent CPA most likely would obtain information about:

    I. Where in the organization chart the internal audit staff reports

   II. The quality of the internal auditors' working paper documentation

(A) I only

(B) II only

(C) Both I and II

(D) Neither I nor II

392. Which of the following factors most likely would assist an independent auditor in assessing the objectivity of the internal auditor?

(A) The professional certifications of the internal audit staff

(B) The consistency of the internal audit reports with the results of work performed

(C) The appropriateness of internal audit conclusions in the circumstances

(D) The organizational status of the director of internal audit

393. During an audit an internal auditor may provide direct assistance to the independent auditor in:

	Performing Tests of Controls	Performing Substantive Tests
(A)	No	Yes
(B)	Yes	No
(C)	No	No
(D)	Yes	Yes

394. An internal auditor who is assessed by the independent auditor to be both competent and objective may assist the independent auditor in the assessment of:

    I. Inherent risk

   II. Control risk

(A) I only

(B) II only

(C) Both I and II

(D) Neither I nor II

395. For which of the following may an independent auditor share responsibility with an entity's internal auditor who is assessed to be both competent and objective?

   I. Materiality levels

  II. Evaluation of accounting estimates

(A) I only

(B) II only

(C) Both I and II

(D) Neither I nor II

396. Which of the following statements is correct about the independent auditor's use of the work of a specialist?

   I. The appropriateness and reasonableness of methods and their application are the responsibility of the specialist.

  II. The auditor is required to perform substantive procedures to verify the specialist's assumptions and findings.

(A) I only

(B) II only

(C) Both I and II

(D) Neither I nor II

397. When an independent auditor hires a specialist to perform certain substantive tests, an understanding should exist among which of the following parties as to the nature of the work to be performed?

   I. The auditor

  II. The client

 III. The specialist

(A) I and II only

(B) I and III only

(C) II and III only

(D) I, II, and III

398. When an independent auditor hires a specialist to perform certain substantive tests and believes that the specialist's findings are reasonable in the circumstances:

   I. The auditor would mention the specialist in the auditor's report

  II. The auditor would either need to be capable of reperforming the specialist's procedures or hire a second specialist to corroborate the findings of the first specialist

(A) I only

(B) II only

(C) Both I and II

(D) Neither I nor II

399. When an independent auditor hires a specialist to perform certain substantive tests:

    I. If the auditor believes that the specialist's findings are contrary to the client's assertions, the auditor would mention the specialist in the auditor's report

    II. If the specialist were related to the client, the auditor would not be able to use that specialist

    (A) I only
    (B) II only
    (C) Both I and II
    (D) Neither I nor II

CHAPTER 13

Ethics, Sarbanes-Oxley, and the COSO Framework

400. According to the AICPA Code of Professional Conduct, Article IV, which of the following is correct regarding objectivity and independence?

(A) Objectivity and independence apply to all services rendered.

(B) Independence applies to all services rendered, but objectivity applies to attestation services only (e.g., audits, special reports, and reviews).

(C) Objectivity applies to all services rendered, but independence applies to attestation services only (e.g., audits, special reports, and reviews).

(D) None of the above

401. According to Rule 101 of the AICPA Code of Professional Conduct, independence will be impaired if a firm does which of the following?

I. Reports to the board on behalf of management

II. Makes operational but not financial decisions for the client

III. Performs nonattest services for an audit client

(A) I and III only

(B) II and III only

(C) I, II, and III

(D) I and II only

402. Which of the following is correct regarding the AICPA Code of Professional Conduct?

I. The AICPA Code of Professional Conduct governs a service that a member of the AICPA performs in the area of compilation and review.

II. The AICPA Code of Professional Conduct does not apply to audits of issuers because Sarbanes-Oxley rules would apply.

(A) I only

(B) II only

(C) Both I and II

(D) Neither I nor II

403. The first three principles (articles) of the AICPA's code of conduct are responsibilities, public interest, and:

(A) Independence
(B) Objectivity
(C) Integrity
(D) Due care

404. According to the AICPA's code of conduct, which of the following areas of professional responsibility should be observed by a CPA not in public practice?

  I. Objectivity
 II. Independence

(A) I only
(B) II only
(C) Both I and II
(D) Neither I nor II

405. Which of the following bodies ordinarily would NOT have the authority to suspend or revoke a CPA's license to practice public accounting?

   I. A state CPA society
  II. The AICPA
 III. A state board of accountancy

(A) I and II only
(B) II and III only
(C) I and III only
(D) III only

406. A violation of the profession's ethical standards most likely would have occurred when a CPA:

  I. Purchased a CPA firm's practice for a percentage of fees to be received over a three-year period
 II. Issued an unmodified opinion on the Year 12 financial statements when fees for the Year 11 audit were unpaid

(A) I only
(B) II only
(C) Both I and II
(D) Neither I nor II

407. Under the ethical standards of the profession, which of the following secured loans is a "permitted loan" regardless of the date it was obtained?

  I. Home mortgage
 II. Automobile loan

(A) I only
(B) II only
(C) Both I and II
(D) Neither I nor II

408. When a CPA leaves his or her firm and joins a client within one year of disassociating from the firm, which of the following applies?

   I. Independence is impaired if a partner or professional employee leaves his or her firm and is employed by a client in a key position even if the individual is no longer in a position to influence or participate in the firm's business.

   II. Independence will be impaired unless the engagement is reviewed by a qualified professional to determine whether the engagement team members maintained the appropriate level of skepticism when evaluating the representations and work of the former firm member.

   (A) I only
   (B) II only
   (C) Both I and II
   (D) Neither I nor II

409. Which of the following fully secured loans, if made today to an auditor, would violate independence standards?

   I. Auto loan
   II. Home mortgage

   (A) I only
   (B) II only
   (C) Both I and II
   (D) Neither I nor II

410. According to the AICPA Code of Professional Conduct, Rule 201— General Standards, which of the following is NOT part of professional competence?

   I. Consulting with others
   II. Ability to supervise and evaluate work

   (A) I only
   (B) II only
   (C) Both I and II
   (D) Neither I nor II

411. Which of the following terms relates to the CPA exercising due professional care?

   I. Reasonably prudent person
   II. Critical review

   (A) I only
   (B) II only
   (C) Both I and II
   (D) Neither I nor II

412. A CPA is NOT allowed to have a fee contingent upon results in which of the following engagements?
   I. Examinations of prospective financial statements
   II. Reviews of historical financial statements
   III. Filing an original tax return, Form 1040

(A) I, II, and III
(B) II and III only
(C) I and III only
(D) I and II only

413. A contingent fee is permissible in which of the following situations?
   I. Review of a nonissuer's historical financial statements
   II. Compilations of financial statements expected to be used by third parties and lack of independence is disclosed in the compilation report
   III. Representation with a client on a previously filed tax return now being audited by the IRS

(A) I and III only
(B) II and III only
(C) II only
(D) III only

414. Which of the following statements best describes the ethical standard of the profession pertaining to advertising and solicitation?
   I. False, misleading, or deceptive advertising is not allowed.
   II. Advertising that is informative and objective is allowed.

(A) I only
(B) II only
(C) Both I and II
(D) Neither I nor II

415. Which of the following is an act discreditable to the profession?
   I. Failure to give working papers to the client after the client makes a demand
   II. Determination by a court or administrative agency of discrimination in public practice

(A) I only
(B) II only
(C) Both I and II
(D) Neither I nor II

416. Which of the following is considered an act discreditable to the profession?
   I. A CPA's failure to return client records to the client because the client has refused to pay the CPA's bill
   II. Disclosing confidential client information during a quality review of a professional practice by a team from the state society of CPAs

(A) I only
(B) II only
(C) Both I and II
(D) Neither I nor II

417. Which of the following would be considered an act discreditable to the profession?
   I. Arranging with a collection agency to collect fees owed by a client
   II. Using an off-site cloud storage server to store confidential client computer files

(A) I only
(B) II only
(C) Both I and II
(D) Neither I nor II

418. A CPA in public practice must be independent when providing which of the following services?
   I. Compilation of a personal financial statement
   II. Compilation of a financial forecast
   III. Attestation engagements

(A) I and III only
(B) II and III only
(C) I, II, and III
(D) III only

419. Under PCAOB, tax services may be provided to an issuer audit client:
   I. Without preapproval from the audit committee
   II. Provided the services do not include aggressive tax transactions

(A) I only
(B) II only
(C) Both I and II
(D) Neither I nor II

420. The AICPA Code of Professional Conduct would be violated if a member reveals confidential client information:

    I. As a result of a validly issued subpoena or summons

    II. As a result of a quality review of the CPA's practice

(A) I only

(B) II only

(C) Both I and II

(D) Neither I nor II

421. According to the Sarbanes-Oxley Act of 2002, only CPA firms registered with PCAOB are permitted to audit:

    I. Privately held entities that do business with issuers of securities

    II. Entities that are issuers of securities

(A) I only

(B) II only

(C) Both I and II

(D) Neither I nor II

422. PCAOB requires a registered CPA firm to:

    I. Provide a concurring or second partner review of each audit report

    II. Describe in the audit reports the extent of the testing of the issuer's internal control structure and procedures

    III. Maintain audit documentation for a minimum of five years

(A) II only

(B) I and II only

(C) I and III only

(D) I only

423. Audit firms need to retain working papers relating to their audit clients for at least:

    I. Seven years if the client is publicly held

    II. Five years if the client is not publicly held

(A) I only

(B) II only

(C) Both I and II

(D) Neither I nor II

424. Under Sarbanes-Oxley, registered audit firms are required to report which of the following information to the audit committee of audited corporations?

    I. A schedule of unadjusted audit differences

   II. The treatment that the audit firm prefers regarding alternative accounting treatments discussed with the corporation's management

(A) I only

(B) II only

(C) Both I and II

(D) Neither I nor II

425. Under PCAOB, a cooling-off period of how many years is required before a member of an issuer's audit engagement team may begin working for the registrant in a key position?

(A) One year

(B) Two years

(C) Three years

(D) Four years

426. According to PCAOB, which of the following must be rotated off an audit engagement every five years?

    I. Lead partner

  II. Reviewing partner

(A) I only

(B) II only

(C) Both I and II

(D) Neither I nor II

427. With regard to auditing a nonissuer, which of the following standards requires lead auditor rotation?

    I. AICPA standards

  II. PCAOB standards

(A) I only

(B) II only

(C) Both I and II

(D) Neither I nor II

428. According to Title VI of Sarbanes-Oxley, which of the following is required as an enhanced financial disclosure?
  I. Any officer, director, or owner of more than 10 percent of any equity security must file a report indicating how many shares they own within 10 days after becoming an officer, director, or more than 10 percent owner.
  II. A change in ownership must be filed within seven days of such change.
  (A) I only
  (B) II only
  (C) Both I and II
  (D) Neither I nor II

429. According to the Sarbanes-Oxley Act of 2002, auditors are required to attest to management's assessment of the effectiveness of internal control over financial reporting in a:
  I. 10-K Annual Report
  II. 10-Q Quarterly Report
  (A) I only
  (B) II only
  (C) Both I and II
  (D) Neither I nor II

430. Firms registered with PCAOB are required to undergo:
  I. PCAOB inspection
  II. Quality review inspection by a peer review panel from the state society
  (A) I only
  (B) II only
  (C) Both I and II
  (D) Neither I nor II

431. Under Sarbanes-Oxley, in an audit of a publicly traded company, the issuer must rotate every five years:
  I. Their designated "financial expert"
  II. Their auditing firm
  (A) I only
  (B) II only
  (C) Both I and II
  (D) Neither I nor II

432. According to Sarbanes-Oxley, an explanation would need to be attached to Forms 10-Q and 10-K if an issuer lacks which of the following?
  I. A financial expert on its audit committee
  II. A code of ethics for senior financial officers

(A) I only
(B) II only
(C) Both I and II
(D) Neither I nor II

433. According to SEC independence rules, independence would be impaired if a partner in the firm provided at least how many hours of nonaudit services to the issuer on a recurring basis?

(A) 1
(B) 10
(C) 40
(D) 100

434. Under Sarbanes-Oxley, after rotating off an audit engagement, lead partners are required to take a "time out" of how many years before returning to an audit engagement?

(A) One year
(B) Two years
(C) Five years
(D) Seven years

435. For a firm that is engaged to audit and is concerned about independence, tax services related to confidential or aggressive tax transactions would be a violation of:
  I. AICPA standards
  II. PCAOB/SEC standards

(A) I only
(B) II only
(C) Both I and II
(D) Neither I nor II

436. Which of the following standards prohibits the performance of financial information system design and implementation services for audit clients?
  I. PCAOB standards relating to audits of issuers
  II. AICPA standards relating to audits of nonissuers

(A) I only
(B) II only
(C) Both I and II
(D) Neither I nor II

437. Which of the following services is a CPA firm NOT allowed to provide to an audit client (issuer of securities), according to Sarbanes-Oxley?
  I.   Bookkeeping services
  II. Income tax return preparation

  (A) I only
  (B) II only
  (C) Both I and II
  (D) Neither I nor II

438. According to Sarbanes-Oxley, which of the following statements is correct regarding an issuer's audit committee's financial expert?
  I.   The audit committee financial expert must be the issuer's audit committee chairperson to enhance internal control.
  II. If an issuer does not have an audit committee financial expert, the issuer must disclose the reason why the role is not filled.

  (A) I only
  (B) II only
  (C) Both I and II
  (D) Neither I nor II

439. Which of the following is correct?
  I.   The PCAOB will inspect the public accounting firms that register with it. If not satisfied by the findings, the PCAOB can revoke the firm's registration so that it cannot audit publicly held companies.
  II. The Public Company Accounting Oversight Board (PCAOB) was established to issue accounting standards for publicly traded companies.

  (A) I only
  (B) II only
  (C) Both I and II
  (D) Neither I nor II

440. Nonaudit services that do not exceed what percentage of total revenues from an audit client do NOT require audit committee preapproval?

  (A) 1
  (B) 2
  (C) 4
  (D) 5

441. The internal control provisions of Sarbanes-Oxley apply to which companies in the United States?

  (A) All public and nonpublic companies
  (B) All public companies
  (C) All issuers with more than 100 stockholders
  (D) All nonissuer companies

442. Regarding internal control, Sarbanes-Oxley requires a publicly traded company to:
  I. Report on their own internal control
  II. Make an assertion regarding the effectiveness of their own internal control
(A) I only
(B) II only
(C) Both I and II
(D) Neither I nor II

443. The most common management tool for evaluating internal control is the:
(A) Sarbanes-Oxley internal control framework
(B) COSO internal framework
(C) AICPA internal control framework
(D) SEC internal control framework

444. According to the COSO internal framework, there are how many components of internal control?
(A) 3
(B) 6
(C) 4
(D) 5

445. The COSO framework of evaluating internal control is recognized as appropriate by:
  I. PCAOB
  II. SEC
(A) I only
(B) II only
(C) Both I and II
(D) Neither I nor II

446. In management's report on internal control (required under Sarbanes-Oxley for a publicly traded company), there is a statement that:
  I. The company's independent auditor has issued an attestation report on management's assertion
  II. Mentions COSO as the framework for evaluating internal control
(A) I only
(B) II only
(C) Both I and II
(D) Neither I nor II

447. Which of the following is required in management's report on internal control under Sarbanes-Oxley?
   I. A statement that management is responsible for internal control
   II. A statement that the independent auditor has assessed management's assertion
   III. Management's assertion of the effectiveness of their internal control

(A) I and III only
(B) I and II only
(C) II and III only
(D) I, II, and III

448. Which of the following is an interrelated component of internal control according to the COSO framework?
   I. Information and communication
   II. Control environment

(A) I only
(B) II only
(C) Both I and II
(D) Neither I nor II

449. Which is NOT one of the interrelated components of internal control according to the COSO framework?
   I. Control activities
   II. Risk assessment

(A) I only
(B) II only
(C) Both I and II
(D) Neither I nor II

450. Regarding internal control under Sarbanes-Oxley, which of the following must be reported to those charged with governance?
   I. All significant deficiencies
   II. All control deficiencies
   III. All material weaknesses

(A) I and III only
(B) II and III only
(C) I and II only
(D) I, II, and III

451. An auditor's communication of material weaknesses and significant deficiencies to those charged with governance should be done:

(A) During the audit and then again at the audit's completion
(B) At the completion of the audit
(C) During the audit
(D) During the audit or at the end of the audit

International Auditing Standards, Government Auditing Standards, and Information Technology

452. With regard to marketing professional services, the International Federation of Accountants (IFAC) indicates that:

(A) Direct marketing is prohibited
(B) Marketing is allowed if lawful
(C) Marketing should be honest and truthful
(D) Marketing of audit services is prohibited

453. In relation to the AICPA Code of Professional Conduct, the IFAC Code of Ethics for Professional Accountants:

(A) Has more outright prohibitions
(B) Has fewer outright prohibitions
(C) Has no outright prohibitions
(D) Applies only to professional accountants in business

454. Which of the following is NOT true about international auditing standards?

  I. The location in which the auditor practices must be disclosed in the audit report.
  II. External confirmation of accounts receivable is generally required.

(A) I only
(B) II only
(C) Both I and II
(D) Neither I nor II

455. Which is correct regarding international auditing standards?
  I. When dating the audit report for a subsequent event, international standards require the dating of the report to be the amended date or a dual date.
  II. If the client suddenly wishes to change the engagement and the auditor is unable to agree with the client as to the reason for the sudden change, the auditor should withdraw and consider whether there is an obligation to contact third parties.

(A) I only
(B) II only
(C) Both I and II
(D) Neither I nor II

456. International financial reporting standards (IFRS) are:
  I. An international alternative to PCAOB audit standards
  II. Accounting standards rather than auditing standards

(A) I only
(B) II only
(C) Both I and II
(D) Neither I nor II

457. Before reporting on the financial statements of a US entity that have been prepared in conformity with another country's accounting principles, an auditor practicing in the United States should:
  I. Understand the accounting principles generally accepted in the other country
  II. Be certified by the appropriate auditing or accounting board of the other country

(A) I only
(B) II only
(C) Both I and II
(D) Neither I nor II

458. With regard to internal audit outsourcing, which of the following is correct?
  I. Permissible under US GAAS for audit clients under certain conditions
  II. Not permissible under international auditing standards for audit clients under any conditions

(A) I only
(B) II only
(C) Both I and II
(D) Neither I nor II

459. Government Auditing Standards published by the United States Government Accountability Office define standards associated with the following types of engagements:
  I. Financial audits
 II. Attest engagements
III. Performance audits

(A) I and III only
(B) I and II only
(C) II and III only
(D) I, II, and III

460. Which of the following is correct regarding reporting requirements in a compliance audit?
  I. The auditor must report on whether the entity has complied with applicable requirements.
 II. The auditor does not express an opinion on the effectiveness of internal control over compliance.

(A) I only
(B) II only
(C) Both I and II
(D) Neither I nor II

461. In performing an audit in accordance with Generally Accepted Government Auditing Standards (the "Yellow Book"), the auditor accepts greater reporting responsibilities than accepted under a GAAS audit, since the auditor must report on:
  I. Compliance with laws, rules, and regulations, violations of which may affect financial statement amounts
 II. The organization's internal control over financial reporting

(A) I only
(B) II only
(C) Both I and II
(D) Neither I nor II

462. Compared to a typical GAAS audit for a for-profit entity, the audit of an entity that receives federal financial assistance requires:
  I. More fieldwork than a typical GAAS audit
 II. Less reporting than a typical GAAS audit

(A) I only
(B) II only
(C) Both I and II
(D) Neither I nor II

463. Which of the following is a documentation requirement that an auditor should follow when auditing in accordance with Government Auditing Standards?
    I. Audit documentation should contain sufficient information so that supplementary oral explanations are not required.
    II. Audit documentation should include the auditor's assessment of the material risk of noncompliance.

    (A) I only
    (B) II only
    (C) Both I and II
    (D) Neither I nor II

464. The auditor's objectives in a compliance audit of a governmental entity include:
    I. Minimizing control risk of noncompliance
    II. Forming an opinion on whether the government complied in all material respects with applicable compliance requirements

    (A) I only
    (B) II only
    (C) Both I and II
    (D) Neither I nor II

465. Auditors engaged to perform a "single audit" of a major program must:
    I. Obtain an understanding of internal control over compliance
    II. Perform tests of controls

    (A) I only
    (B) II only
    (C) Both I and II
    (D) Neither I nor II

466. Auditors engaged to perform a single audit must perform procedures to obtain an understanding of internal control pertaining to the compliance requirements for federal programs sufficient to plan an audit and to support a low assessed level of control risk for:
    I. Major programs
    II. Nonmajor programs

    (A) I only
    (B) II only
    (C) Both I and II
    (D) Neither I nor II

467. Under the Single Audit Act, auditors are responsible for:
  I. Understanding internal control
  II. Reporting the results of their tests

(A) I only
(B) II only
(C) Both I and II
(D) Neither I nor II

468. In which of the following audits is the CPA required to prepare a written report on the auditor's understanding of internal control and the assessment of control risk?
  I. Audits performed in accordance with GAGAS
  II. Audits performed in accordance with GAAS

(A) I only
(B) II only
(C) Both I and II
(D) Neither I nor II

469. Reporting responsibilities under GAGAS are expanded to include·
  I. Reports on compliance with laws, rules, and regulations
  II. Reports on internal control over financial reporting

(A) I only
(B) II only
(C) Both I and II
(D) Neither I nor II

470. Which of the following is correct regarding program-specific audits under the Single Audit Act?
  I. Program-specific audits do not involve reporting on the financial statements of the entity spending federal financial assistance.
  II. If the entity spending federal financial assistance does not meet certain criteria, a program-specific audit must be performed rather than a single audit.

(A) I only
(B) II only
(C) Both I and II
(D) Neither I nor II

471. Which of the following best describes a single audit?

(A) An audit of federal financial assistance
(B) A report on fair presentation of financial statements
(C) A combined audit of both an entity's financial statements and federal financial assistance programs
(D) A program-specific audit

472. Which of the following is an engagement attribute for an audit of an entity that processes most of its financial data in electronic form without any paper documentation?

I. Increased effort to search for evidence of management fraud
II. Performance of audit tests on a continuous basis

(A) I only
(B) II only
(C) Both I and II
(D) Neither I nor II

473. Durka Company, a client of Corey, CPA, has recently automated its accounting system. While Corey has been the auditor of Durka for several years, this will be the first audit encompassing the new system. Which of the following is most likely a result of this change?

I. Corey will need to take courses to develop an appropriate level of IT skill.
II. Corey will need to revise his audit objectives from prior years to reflect the new situation.
III. Corey will need to revise his audit program and audit procedures from prior years to reflect the new situation.

(A) III only
(B) I and II only
(C) II and III only
(D) I, II, and III

474. The Malkin Corp. has recently installed a new computerized payroll-processing program. Before the program is used to compute actual payroll checks for the employees, test data are going to be run through the computer to see how they would be processed. Which of the following is likely to be tested in this manner?

I. Two checks requested for the same employee
II. A check requested for an employee who hasn't worked for the company in two months

(A) I only
(B) II only
(C) Both I and II
(D) Neither I nor II

475. Which of the following controls involves dummy transactions being run simultaneously with live transactions in the client's computer system?
  I. Test data
  II. Integrated test facility

(A) I only
(B) II only
(C) Both I and II
(D) Neither I nor II

476. Which of the following is a computer-assisted audit technique that permits an auditor to insert the auditor's version of a client's program to process data and compare the output with the client's output?
  I. Test data
  II. Parallel simulation

(A) I only
(B) II only
(C) Both I and II
(D) Neither I nor II

477. An auditor would likely use generalized audit software to:
  I.   Construct parallel simulations
  II. Assess IT control risk
  III. Access client data files

(A) I and II only
(B) I and III only
(C) I, II, and III
(D) III only

CHAPTER 15

Management Representation Letter and Quality Control at the Firm

478. Which of the following is true regarding the management representation letter under US GAAS and PCAOB?
   I. The date of the management rep letter should match the date of the auditor's report.
   II. Under certain circumstances, failure to obtain a management representation letter is not a scope limitation.

   (A) I only
   (B) II only
   (C) Both I and II
   (D) Neither I nor II

479. Under US GAAS, which of the following officers would need to sign the management rep letter?
   I. CEO
   II. CFO

   (A) I only
   (B) II only
   (C) Both I and II
   (D) Neither I nor II

480. With respect to the management rep letter, materiality would apply to management having made available to the auditor access to which of the following?
   I. Minutes of board meetings
   II. Records relating to revenue and expenses

   (A) I only
   (B) II only
   (C) Both I and II
   (D) Neither I nor II

481. In a typical management representation letter, management would acknowledge their responsibility for:
    I. Fair presentation of financial statements
    II. Internal control over financial reporting
    III. Communicating to the audit committee any material disagreements with the auditor
    (A) I and II only
    (B) I, II, and III
    (C) I only
    (D) II only

482. Which of the following should be found in the management representation letter?
    I. The results of management's assessment of the risk that the financial statements may be materially misstated due to fraud
    II. A statement that all known or potential litigation has been disclosed to the auditor
    (A) I only
    (B) II only
    (C) Both I and II
    (D) Neither I nor II

483. The following quote is found in the current file from a communication pertaining to an audit of financial statements.

    ". . . There are no material transactions that have not been properly recorded in the accounting records underlying the financial statements. . . ."

    Which communication is the quote likely to be taken from?
    (A) Management representation letter
    (B) Communication with predecessor auditor
    (C) Auditor's engagement letter
    (D) Auditor's report

484. The following quote is found in the current file from a communication pertaining to an audit of financial statements.

    ". . . Fees for our services are based on our per diem rates plus travel expenses. . . ."

    Which communication is the quote likely to be taken from?
    (A) Auditor's report
    (B) Audit inquiry letter to legal counsel
    (C) Engagement letter
    (D) Management representation letter

485. The following quote is found in the current file from a communication pertaining to an audit of financial statements.

"... The objective of our audit is to express an opinion on the financial statements, although it is possible that facts or circumstances encountered may prevent us from expressing an unmodified opinion. ..."

   Which communication is the quote likely to be taken from?
   (A) Engagement letter
   (B) Management representation letter
   (C) Auditor's inquiry to client's legal counsel
   (D) Communication with predecessor auditor

486. The following quote is found in the current file from a communication pertaining to an audit of financial statements.

"... There has been no fraud involving employees that could have a material effect on the financial statements. ..."

   Which communication is the quote likely to be taken from?
   (A) Communication with audit committee
   (B) Audit inquiry letter to legal counsel
   (C) Management representation letter
   (D) Communication with the predecessor

487. The following quote is found in the current file from a communication pertaining to an audit of financial statements.

"... Are you aware of any facts or circumstances that may indicate a lack of integrity by any member of senior management? ..."

   Which communication is the quote likely to be taken from?
   (A) Management representation letter
   (B) Engagement letter
   (C) Auditor's report
   (D) Communication with predecessor auditor

488. The following quote is found in the current file from a communication pertaining to an audit of financial statements.

"... There were unreasonable delays by management in permitting the start of the audit and in providing needed information. ..."

   Which communication is the quote likely to be taken from?
   (A) External receivable confirmation
   (B) Auditor's engagement letter
   (C) Auditor's communication with audit committee
   (D) Management representation letter

489. The following quote is found in the current file from a communication pertaining to an audit of financial statements.

". . . If this statement is not correct, please write promptly, using the enclosed envelope, and give details of any differences directly to our auditors. . . ."

Which communication is the quote likely to be taken from?

(A) External receivable confirmation
(B) Management representation letter
(C) Audit inquiry to legal counsel
(D) Communication with predecessor

490. The following quote is found in the current file from a communication pertaining to an audit of financial statements.

". . . The company has suffered recurring losses from operations and has a net capital deficiency that raises substantial doubt about its ability to continue as a going concern. . . ."

Which communication is the quote likely to be taken from?

(A) Audit inquiry letter to legal counsel
(B) External receivable confirmation
(C) Communication with predecessor
(D) Auditor's report

491. Which of the following requires a CPA firm providing audit and attest services to adopt a system of quality control?

  I. AICPA
 II. IRS

(A) I only
(B) II only
(C) Both I and II
(D) Neither I nor II

492. Which of the following elements of quality control encompasses criteria for recruitment and hiring compensation and advancement?

(A) Leadership responsibilities
(B) Human resources
(C) Risk assessment
(D) Monitoring

493. Which of the following is NOT one of the interrelated elements of quality control at the firm?

(A) Considering audit risk
(B) Leadership responsibilities
(C) Client acceptance and continuance
(D) Monitoring

494. With regard to the elements of quality control at the firm, the category known as leadership responsibilities is essential because:

I. The firm's leadership bears the ultimate responsibility for the firm's quality control systems

II. The firm must be able to perform the engagement within the reporting deadlines

(A) I only
(B) II only
(C) Both I and II
(D) Neither I nor II

495. When measuring the quality control at a CPA firm, providing a means to resolve differences of opinion falls under the category of:

(A) Performance
(B) Leadership
(C) Monitoring
(D) Human resources

496. With regard to a firm's system of quality control, which component of quality control involves an ongoing consideration and evaluation of the design and effectiveness of the quality control system?

(A) Performance
(B) Leadership
(C) Monitoring
(D) Human resources

497. With regard to quality control, Sarbanes-Oxley requires for every public company audit:

I. Peer review to be conducted under the AICPA standards so that one firm may review another firm's quality control system

II. A wrap-up or secondary partner review of the audit documentation by a partner not otherwise involved in the audit

(A) I only
(B) II only
(C) Both I and II
(D) Neither I nor II

498. A CPA firm that fails to maintain quality control standards:

I. Has not necessarily violated generally accepted auditing standards

II. May still be in compliance with professional standards with respect to individual engagements

(A) I only
(B) II only
(C) Both I and II
(D) Neither I nor II

499. The CPA firm's size as well as cost-benefit considerations should be taken into account when:
   I. Determining independence with respect to a client
   II. Developing quality controls at the CPA firm
   (A) I only
   (B) II only
   (C) Both I and II
   (D) Neither I nor II

500. Which of the following is correct regarding client quality-control standards at the firm?
   I. Quality-control standards apply to auditing and attestation but not to accounting and review.
   II. A primary purpose of quality-control standards is to minimize the likelihood of associating with a client whose management lacks integrity.
   (A) I only
   (B) II only
   (C) Both I and II
   (D) Neither I nor II

Bonus Questions

501. Regarding assurance engagements under IFAC, which of the following standards helps to ensure independence?
   I. Lead partners should be rotated off the engagement every five years.
   II. Lead partners should take a "time-out" for two years before returning to lead the engagement.
   (A) I only
   (B) II only
   (C) Both I and II
   (D) Neither I nor II

502. According to AICPA and PCAOB standards, which of the following loans in the amount of $20,000 from a financial institution audit client to a CPA would impair the CPA's independence?
   (A) Cash advance of $20,000 collateralized by money market cash deposits in the same financial institution of $27,000
   (B) Auto loan of $20,000 from a financial institution audit client, made under normal lending policies
   (C) Cash advance from a financial institution of $20,000 to be repaid within 10 days, made under normal lending policies
   (D) All of the above

Chapter 1: Proper Use of the Term *Audit* and an Overview of Auditing

1. (A) I is correct. While the Public Company Accounting Oversight Board (PCAOB) sets the standards for audits of publicly traded entities, the Auditing Standards Board continues to set the standards with regard to audits of financial statements of nonissuers. Auditors of nonissuers are required to comply with Statements on Auditing Standards and should be prepared to justify any departures. II is wrong. PCAOB is empowered under the Sarbanes-Oxley Act of 2002 to set auditing standards with regard to publicly traded companies (issuers).

2. (B) II is correct. Whenever an independent expert is brought in to examine financial statements with hopes of adding credibility, that engagement and reporting process is known as an attestation but NOT necessarily an audit because there are several types of attestations. I is wrong. When an attestation is carried out on historic financial information, the attestation is known as an audit. There is no indication in the question that the financial statements are historic; therefore, the term *attestation* may be used but NOT the term *audit*. An audit is the highest level of attestation service a CPA may provide.

3. (C) I is correct. When an attestation is carried out on historic financial information, the attestation is known as an audit. An audit is the highest level of attestation service a CPA may provide. It involves providing an opinion, and, therefore, the CPA must be independent. It is important to note that an audit is just one type of attestation. Use the term *audit* when the CPA is doing an attestation engagement involving historic financial statements. II is correct. While audits are attestations that look backward at historic financial information, examination engagements are attestations that look forward. Therefore, when the CPA examines in Year 3 what Year 4 may look like, this is an example of an attestation but not an audit. The CPA Exam expects a candidate to know the proper use of the word *audit*.

4. (B) II is correct. Financial statements are the responsibility of the management of the reporting organization. The responsibility of the independent auditor is to express an opinion on those statements based on an audit. I is wrong. Even after the audit is completed and the opinion expressed, financial statements are still the responsibility of the management of the reporting organization. The responsibility of the independent auditor is to express an opinion on those statements based on an audit.

5. (D) I is wrong. In the auditor's report, consistency of accounting principles from period to period is implied and only referred to explicitly if there is an inconsistency. For example, if the client used FIFO in Year 1 for inventory valuation, it's implied that he or she also used FIFO in Year 2. This would be consistent and, therefore, would NOT have to be expressed in the auditor's report. However, if the client used FIFO in Year 1 and Average Cost in Year 2, this would represent an inconsistency and would need to be expressed in the report. II is wrong. In an auditor's standard report the fact that client disclosures and footnotes are adequate need not be indicated. The auditor would mention disclosures and footnotes only if there were problems with them. Otherwise, it is implied in a standard audit report that client footnotes and disclosures are adequate.

6. (D) I is wrong. Family members employed by the audit client do not automatically affect the independence of a covered member. A spouse of a covered member can work for the company under audit as long as there is no influence on the financial statements. II is wrong. A dependent child of a covered member can work for the client under audit, without impairing independence, provided there is no influence on financial statements. Jobs that would impair independence include accounting jobs like internal auditor or controller, or any job that influences the financial activities of the client.

7. (B) II is correct. For covered members and their families, there are direct ownership rules and there are indirect ownership rules when it comes to owning stocks and bonds of the client company. Although direct ownership rules are very specific, indirect ownership rules are less specific. Indirect ownership results from owning shares in a mutual fund, and the mutual fund owns shares in the client company. If the spouse of a covered member owns an immaterial number of shares in a mutual fund, and the mutual fund happens to own shares of the client company, the indirect immaterial financial interest is OK and would not impair independence. I is wrong. Direct ownership rules are very specific and materiality is NOT a factor. If the spouse or dependent of a covered member owns even one share of stock directly in the client company, independence is impaired regardless of the child's age. Independence would be impaired whether the shares were held in a brokerage account or in a safe-deposit box.

8. (A) I is correct. Materiality would not apply, since the audit firm itself is considered a covered member and independence would be impaired. While ownership of one share is clearly immaterial, an audit firm is not allowed to own any shares of its client under audit. II is incorrect. Materiality would apply to indirect ownership of just a single share in a mutual fund. The spouse of a covered member may not directly own any shares, but, indirectly, through a mutual fund, an immaterial indirect ownership is allowed.

9. (B) II is correct. An audit firm cannot have unpaid audit fees from the previous year when it issues an audit report for the current year. The audit can still take place and all the fieldwork can be done, but no opinion can be given until payment is received from the prior year's audit. I is wrong. If a dependent of a covered member is employed as a parking lot attendant of the client under audit, this would not by itself impair independence. Only if the spouse or immediate family member of a covered member were employed at the client in a position that could influence the financial statements would independence be impaired.

10. (B) II is correct. An auditor is required to document the auditor's understanding of the client's internal control structure. This documentation may be in the form of a flowchart or questionnaire. Documenting the auditor's understanding of internal control is an important fieldwork standard. I is wrong. Under generally accepted auditing standards, the auditor is not required to test controls in an audit of a nonissuer. If the client were a publicly traded company (issuer), then the auditor would be required to test controls, but the question clearly indicates that the client is a nonissuer.

11. (C) I is correct. In an examination of forward-looking financial information, the independent CPA gathers evidence and then provides an opinion regarding fair presentation of the forward-looking information. II is correct. In an audit, the independent CPA gathers evidence and then provides an opinion regarding fair presentation of the historic financial information. Remember, both audits and examinations are attestations. Attestations involve a high level of service; therefore, the CPA must be independent. The term *audit* is used to describe the attestation engagement when the financial information is historic.

Chapter 2: Audit Planning and Risk Assessment

12. (C) I is correct. The CPA needs to assess the auditability of the client by considering the adequacy of the accounting records. Lack of quality accounting records equals a scope limitation. Sometimes an auditor can work within the scope limitation, but the auditor would want to know about this before accepting the engagement. II is correct. The auditor needs to know the future plans for the company because they may impact the decision whether to accept the engagement. Before accepting an engagement, the auditor should determine why the company even needs an audit. For example, are they considering going public? Sometimes a bank demands an audit be performed in order to renew the client's loan or line of credit.

13. (C) I is correct. Inquiries of the predecessor prior to acceptance of the audit engagement should include specific questions regarding facts that might bear on the integrity of management. II is correct. Inquiries of the predecessor prior to acceptance should include any disagreements that the predecessor had with management as to accounting principles and procedures. Other significant matters should be addressed with the predecessor auditor also, such as communications with those charged with governance regarding fraud, conforming with laws and regulations, and the predecessor's understanding as to the reasons for the change of auditors.

14. (D) I is wrong. If a CPA lacks an understanding of the client's industry and accounting principles but feels confident that such information and knowledge can be obtained prior to commencement of the audit, the engagement can still be accepted. II is wrong. If the client's management has unusually high turnover, the engagement can still be accepted, although the high turnover would be considered a fraud risk factor.

15. (A) I is correct. Obtaining a signed engagement letter from the client's management spelling out the understanding between the client and the CPA is essential in the planning stage. The engagement letter is the most common form of written understanding between client and CPA. II is wrong. Examining documents to detect illegal acts having a material effect on the financial statements is considered evidence gathering. Evidence gathering is not likely to be done in the planning stage and is more likely to be done later in the audit. *Exam hint:* The Auditing and Attestation section of the CPA Exam often asks questions that involve audit procedures and when they are to be performed. This question asks about the planning stage and what procedures are to be performed during planning. The correct answer involves an engagement letter because a written understanding is a procedure to be performed in the planning stage. The incorrect answer is often a necessary audit procedure but performed in a different stage of the audit. There are many questions similar to this style throughout the Auditing and Attestation section where the wrong answer involves a correct audit procedure performed in a different part of the audit.

16. (A) I is correct. Procedures likely to be performed in the planning stage of an audit include determining the extent of involvement, if any, of consultants, specialists, and internal auditors. II is wrong. External confirmation of accounts receivable balances is a substantive test, performed in the evidence-gathering stage of the audit.

17. (C) Although an understanding with the audit client must be in writing, an engagement letter is not mandatory. An engagement letter is standard practice, but other formats may be used, provided all responsibilities of the auditor and management are clearly presented. Compare with review and compilation, where the understanding with the client must be in the form of an engagement letter. A is wrong. The responsibilities should cover the auditor's responsibilities, that the auditor is responsible for an opinion regarding the financial statements being prepared in conformity with the framework. B is wrong. Limitations of the engagement should be included in the understanding with the client. An example of limitations would be the following: "Our engagement is subject to the risk that material errors and fraud may exist and will not be detected." D is wrong. The written understanding should include the audit fee and frequency of billing to minimize misunderstandings.

18. (D) I is correct. The engagement letter should state that management is responsible for the financial statements and for adjusting the financial statements to correct material misstatements identified by the auditor. II is correct. The engagement letter should state that management is responsible for compliance with laws and regulations. III is correct. The engagement letter should state that management is responsible for selection and application of accounting policies. The engagement letter should also state that management is responsible for internal controls, making all financial records available to the auditor, and providing the auditor with a representation letter at the end of the audit.

19. (B) II is correct. The auditor makes a preliminary judgment about materiality in the planning stage of the audit based on annualized interim financial statements, which the auditor reads during the planning stage. I is wrong. The auditor makes a preliminary judgment of materiality in the planning stage. An internal control questionnaire applies to the internal control stage of the audit, not the planning stage. *Exam hint:* The Auditing and Attestation section of the CPA Exam is centered around knowing which procedures are done in which stages of the audit. If it's a planning question, and the answer choice says something about an internal control procedure, it is the wrong answer. Internal control happens after the planning stage.

20. (B) II is correct. Coordinating the assistance of entity personnel in data preparation is usually performed during the planning stage. III is correct. During planning, the auditor generally would read the current year's interim financial statements. I is wrong. Selecting a sample of vendors' invoices for comparison to receiving reports is performed during the evidence-gathering stage of the audit.

21. (C) I is correct. Complex transactions would cause an auditor to assess inherent risk as high. For example, if it were difficult for the auditor to understand the point at which the earnings process is complete, the auditor would assess inherent risk as high. III is correct. Relying heavily on estimates allows management the opportunity to be biased in making those estimates. An auditor would likely assess inherent risk as high if many figures are based on estimates rather than actual figures. Estimations are less open to objective verification. Therefore, the possibility of a material misstatement occurring is usually greater for figures that must be estimated. When the auditor is evaluating an account where significant estimations are reported, the degree of inherent risk is usually assessed at a relatively high level. II is wrong. Many related-party transactions would cause an auditor to assess inherent risk as high. The auditor would rather discover that no related-party transactions have taken place because the auditor fears that management will disguise related-party transactions and make them appear arm's-length. The more related-party transactions, the higher the assessed level of inherent risk.

22. (B) II is correct. Inherent risk is assessed by the auditor, but this assessment has no bearing on the actual amount of inherent risk present and the auditor can do nothing to mitigate the amount of inherent risk that is present. I is wrong. Since the auditor's assessment of inherent risk has no bearing on the actual level of inherent risk, inherent risk exists independent of the financial statement audit. Inherent risk is a characteristic of the accounting system and the personnel who work in that system.

23. (A) I is correct. Inherent risk is assessed by the auditor. Inherent risk represents the risk that there are material errors in the financial statements. An auditor assesses inherent risk as high or low based on factors such as transactions being complex and difficult for the auditor to understand. Other factors that have an impact on the auditor's assessment of inherent risk relate to whether there are many related-party transactions and client-prepared estimates substituting for actual amounts in the financial statements. Inherent risk is assessed early in the audit, in the planning stage. II is wrong. Control risk is assessed by the auditor in the internal control stage, not the planning stage. Control risk can be assessed as high if the auditor feels that the client's internal controls will not prevent or detect a material misstatement.

24. (C) I is correct. Control risk is assessed by the auditor after coming to an understanding and documenting the five components of internal control. The auditor's assessment, although based on judgment, has no bearing on how good or bad the client's controls actually are. The more work that went into the auditor's assessment—testing controls and so on—the more likely that the auditor came to the correct assessment of control risk. However, the auditor's assessment of control risk has nothing to do with the amount of control risk present. The auditor's assessment of control risk does not affect the chance that the client's internal controls will fail to detect or prevent a material error from appearing on the financial statements. The auditor's assessment is simply the auditor's judgment of how much risk the auditor thinks he or she is facing. II is correct. Inherent risk is assessed by the auditor, and, once again, the auditor's assessment has no bearing on the actual amount of inherent risk present. Inherent risk is the risk that a material error will not be prevented or detected on a timely basis so that the misstatement will wind up on the financial statements. The auditor's assessment is simply the auditor's judgment of how much risk the auditor thinks he or she is facing.

25. (C) I is correct. Detection risk is a component of audit risk. Audit risk is made up of inherent risk, control risk, and detection risk. II is correct. Inherent risk is a component of audit risk.

26. (C) If inherent risk and control risk are assessed as high by the auditor, this would result in the auditor thinking that he or she is facing high risk that the financial statements contain material misstatements. This would make it more difficult for the auditor to give reasonable assurance that the financial statements are presented in conformity with the framework. In that situation, the auditor's best chance of lowering overall audit risk would be to lower detection risk, being more careful when performing substantive testing. A and B are wrong. The auditor cannot reduce inherent risk or control risk, as the auditor only assesses inherent risk and control risk.

27. (A) An increase in the assessed level of control risk means that the assessed risk of material misstatement has also increased, and this requires a corresponding decrease in detection risk to maintain the same (presumably low) level of overall audit risk. Increasing the extent of tests of details will result in a reduction in detection risk and thus reduce overall audit risk. B is wrong. If the auditor increased the assessed level of control risk, the result would be an increase in the extent of tests of details, not a decrease. C is wrong. An auditor cannot increase or decrease inherent risk; an auditor only assesses inherent risk. D is wrong. In an audit under GAAS, an auditor does not perform tests of controls if the assessed level of inherent risk is high.

28. (B) II is correct. Detection risk is part of overall audit risk, but detection risk is not assessed by the auditor. Rather, detection risk is lowered or raised by the auditor. I is wrong. Control risk is part of overall audit risk, and control risk is assessed by the auditor.

29. (C) I is correct. Inherent risk is a client characteristic that is evaluated by the auditor. The more work and testing done by the auditor, the better the chances that the evaluation will be accurate. II is correct. The quantity of work performed by the auditor will not impact the actual amount of inherent risk present within the reporting company; it is a characteristic of the accounting system and the personnel who work in that system.

30. (B) II is correct. Good internal controls at the client company can mitigate the client's control risk. I is wrong. The quantity of work performed by the auditor during the internal control stage of the audit will not impact the actual amount of control risk present within the reporting company. Control risk is a client characteristic that must be assessed by the auditor.

31. (C) I is correct. The assessments of inherent and control risk will vary inversely with the level of detection risk that is considered to be acceptable. If inherent risk and control risk are both estimated as being high for a particular account or assertion, detection risk must be reduced to a level where overall audit risk is at an acceptable level. Only then would the auditor be able to provide reasonable assurance that the financial statements are in conformity with the reporting framework. II is correct. As a result of lowering detection risk, more substantive testing and more evidence gathering will be needed.

32. (C) I is correct. The amount and type of evidence that is gathered by the auditor will influence the level of detection risk. More evidence will reduce the detection risk as will gathering evidence of a better quality. II and III are wrong. Inherent risk and control risk are company characteristics that are assessed by the auditor. They are not affected by the work performed by the auditor.

33. (D) II is correct. The auditor's decision to reduce detection risk ultimately reduces overall audit risk. I is wrong. An auditor cannot reduce control risk. An auditor can only assess control risk. III is wrong. An auditor cannot reduce inherent risk. An auditor can only assess inherent risk.

34. (A) I is correct. Testing that uses more sophisticated techniques or more experienced auditors will, indeed, generate evidence that is considered of a better quality. II is wrong. Evidence gathered closer to the end of the year will be considered superior to evidence obtained at an earlier point in time. This is because the auditor is rendering an opinion on the year-end balances, not balances at earlier times during the year. Therefore, evidence gathered at year-end is considered better evidence to support the auditor's opinion of year-end balances.

35. (A) Overall audit risk is made up of the risk of material misstatement and detection risk. The risk of material misstatement is itself comprised of two separate risks, inherent risk and control risk. When the assessed level of control risk is increased, the risk of material misstatement also increases, and detection risk must be decreased to achieve an overall audit risk level that is substantially the same as the planned audit risk level. Therefore, B, C, and D are wrong.

36. (C) Inherent risk is the susceptibility of a material misstatement, assuming there are no related controls. A is wrong. The auditor does not assess inherent risk in order to assist the internal auditor's communications to the audit committee. B is wrong. The risk that the internal control system will not detect a material misstatement of a financial statement assertion is known as control risk. D is wrong. The risk that the audit procedures implemented will not detect a material misstatement of a financial statement assertion is known as nonsampling risk.

37. (C) I is correct. There is an inverse relationship between detection risk and the auditor's assessment of inherent risk. Detection risk needs to be lowered when inherent risk is assessed as high. The result of assessing inherent and control risk as high is that more substantive tests would be needed. II is correct. There is an inverse relationship between detection risk and the auditor's assessment of control risk. Detection risk needs to be lowered when control risk is assessed as high. The result is that more substantive tests would be needed. Detection risk has an inverse relationship with both inherent risk and control risk. If control risk and inherent risk are assessed as high, detection risk needs to be lowered. By lowering detection risk, the auditor would be attempting to be more careful than usual.

38. (B) II is correct. Overstating ending inventory by changing count tags is an example of fraudulent financial reporting. I is wrong. Stealing assets is an example of misappropriation. There are two types of fraud, fraudulent financial reporting and misappropriation. If the question asks about one type, make sure you don't choose the other. While both I and II are examples of fraud, the question asks which one is fraudulent financial reporting.

39. (B) II is correct. The recording of false sales prior to year-end to help reach company sales forecasts is an example of fraudulent financial reporting. I is wrong. The treasurer stealing cash is fraud, but stealing cash is an example of misappropriation of assets, not fraudulent financial reporting.

40. (A) I is correct. An error is an unintentional mistake, whereas fraud is an intentional action that distorts the financial statements. The problem here with the application of the accounting principle seems to be unintentional and could have been caused by an accident. II is wrong. Fraud would be an intentional rather than unintentional misstatement. Knowledge of the intention behind the misstatement would be necessary to distinguish between an error and an act of fraud.

41. (B) I, II, and III are all correct. Special consideration must be given to the possibility that fraud exists during the auditor's assessment of inherent risk and control risk and during the auditor's substantive testing.

42. (C) I is correct. Unauthorized client transactions are a fraud risk factor. If the auditor finds unauthorized client transactions and other fraud risk factors, the auditor would raise the assessment of inherent risk, and, as a result, the auditor would possibly have to lower detection risk. II is correct. Unusual client delays is a fraud risk factor. If the client takes a significant amount of time responding to auditor inquiries, the auditor would have to increase the assessment of inherent risk and possibly have to lower detection risk. Fraud risk factors are situations or events that increase the possibility that fraud has occurred. Fraud may not be present, but the chances are elevated. Fraud risk factors include missing documents, unauthorized transactions, and unusual delays. If these factors are encountered, the auditor will probably have to do more extensive substantive procedures or more specialized testing.

43. (A) I is correct. Whenever optimistic earnings forecasts are issued, company officials may feel pressure to achieve those projections. If net income does not materialize as anticipated, the company may revert to fraudulent financial reporting (such as the recording of false sales) to reach the amounts that were promised. II is wrong. The auditor expects all requests for documents to be delivered completely and timely; if not, this would be a fraud risk factor.

44. (A) I is correct. The threat of bankruptcy is a fraud risk factor. The company may be engaging in hiding assets from creditors or stealing assets so that the assets won't become part of a bankruptcy estate. Another fraud risk factor in bankruptcy is fraudulent financial reporting to make the company's balance sheet appear better. II is wrong. The presence, not the absence, of significant competition would represent a fraud risk factor.

45. (C) I is correct. The auditor would test for improper revenue recognition due to fraud by possibly comparing sales volume with production capacity. An excess of sales over production capacity may be indicative of the recording of fictitious sales. II is correct. The auditor would test overstatement of revenue by comparing sales in one month with sales returns in the following month. Larger than average sales in one month compared to larger than average sales returns in the following month would be an indication of overstating revenue.

46. (C) Both I and II are correct. The fraud triangle is comprised of three legs: (1) the incentive or pressure to commit fraud, (2) the opportunity to commit fraud, and (3) the ability to rationalize fraud. The more legs of the fraud triangle that are present in a given situation, the greater the risk of fraud.

47. (D) II is correct. The decision to go public could easily result in additional pressure to commit fraudulent financial reporting in order to attract investors and receive the highest possible IPO price. III is correct. Whenever optimistic earnings forecasts are issued, company officials may feel pressure to achieve those projections. If net income does not materialize as anticipated, the company may resort to fraudulent financial reporting (such as the recording of false sales) to reach the amounts that were promised. I is wrong. Large amounts of cash would be a fraud risk factor regarding misappropriation, not fraudulent financial reporting.

48. (C) I is correct. Significant, unusual, or highly complex transactions occurring near the end of the year provide an opportunity to commit fraudulent financial reporting. If determined, the auditor would likely reduce detection risk as a result and examine these transactions more carefully. II is correct. Having a number of reported balances based on significant estimations provides an opportunity to commit fraudulent financial reporting. If determined, the auditor would likely raise the assessed level of inherent risk. This doesn't mean that there is fraud, but management may be biased with the estimates, and the financial statements could be misstated as a result. The auditor would likely reduce detection risk as a result.

49. (D) I is wrong. High turnover of senior management would create an opportunity to commit fraudulent financial reporting but would not be an incentive. Incentives to commit fraudulent financial reporting would come from members of management or other employees facing pressures that make fraud more likely. For example, if employees are scheduled to receive bonuses based on the stock price or reported net income, they have an incentive to make the company results look especially good. Also, employees may have their own personal financial pressures. II is wrong. Unreasonable demands on the independent auditor is a fraud risk factor that indicates that individuals within the company have the attitude needed to commit fraud and are in a position to rationalize such false reporting. Unreasonable demands placed upon the auditor are not an incentive to commit fraudulent reporting.

50. (A) I is correct. Declining demand and a shrinking industry result in lower sales and would add to the pressure or incentive to commit fraudulent financial reporting. II is correct. Negative cash flows from operations could also create pressure to commit fraudulent financial reporting. Inability to generate cash flows from operations while somehow reporting substantial earnings growth would be a fraud risk factor for fraudulent financial reporting. III is correct. If the company were seeking debt financing, higher interest rates would be charged if the company were shown to have a high risk for default. The incentive for fraudulent financial reporting would be increased in order to make the company look like a better credit risk.

51. (C) I is correct. Insider buying of company shares would NOT heighten the auditor's concern about fraudulent financial reporting. Insider selling is more likely to be viewed as a fraud risk factor. III is correct. An auditor would expect management to be dominated by several top executives. If management were dominated by only one or two top executives, that could be a fraud risk factor as anytime one person can override internal controls, there is opportunity for fraud. IV is correct. Although small high-value inventory items create an opportunity to steal, the question asks about fraudulent financial reporting, not misappropriation of assets. II is wrong. If management placed substantial emphasis on meeting earnings projections, this would be a fraud risk factor relating to pressure to commit fraudulent financial reporting.

52. (D) I is correct. The best place to start looking for fraud is in the planning stage, where the auditor first brainstorms with the audit team and begins to identify potential fraud and fraud risk factors. II is correct. During the internal control stage, the auditor can identify specific controls that can minimize the risk from those fraud risk factors previously identified in the planning stage. Brainstorming sessions could continue to reveal fraud risk factors in the internal control stage. III is correct. An auditor will still be looking for fraud even as late as the evidence-gathering stage. Some fraud is very well hidden. The higher up the fraud exists, the more difficult it is for the auditor to detect.

53. (A) III is correct. An overly complex organization structure involving unusual lines of authority provides an opportunity for fraudulent financial reporting that would heighten the auditor's concern. I is wrong. Large amounts of liquid assets that are easily convertible into cash would heighten an auditor's concern about misappropriation of assets, not about fraudulent financial reporting. II is wrong. Financial management is expected to participate in the selection of accounting principles. Perhaps if nonfinancial management participated in the selection of accounting principles, that might heighten the auditor's concern, but that is not what the question asks.

54. (D) I is wrong. Although collusion makes fraud more difficult to detect, the audit should be designed to detect material errors and fraud, regardless of the cause. The presence of employee collusion does not change the auditor's responsibility, but it may affect certain audit procedures. II is wrong. An auditor is responsible for designing the audit to provide reasonable assurance of detecting material misstatement. This responsibility is the same regardless of the cause of the misstatement. Management override of controls might explain why a properly planned and executed audit did not result in the discovery of material fraud, but the presence of management override does not change the auditor's responsibility.

55. (C) The auditor should assess the risk that errors and fraud may cause the financial statements to contain a material misstatement. Based on that assessment, the auditor should design the audit to provide reasonable assurance of detecting material errors and fraud. A, B, and D all contain exclusions that are incorrect.

56. (D) These two situations are fraud risk factors that would indicate to the independent CPA that there is an incentive for employees or pressure on employees to misappropriate assets. High personal debts and layoffs would make employees feel more pressure to steal from the company to protect their families. As a result, companies sometimes screen potential employees by asking questions regarding personal credit card debt. A is wrong. An incentive to commit fraudulent financial reporting would involve a company that is about to issue stock or bonds and that is feeling the pressure to "cook the books" for a lower interest rate or higher IPO price. B is wrong. An example of an opportunity to commit misappropriation of assets would be if a company lacked safeguards over assets. An auditor would be concerned about misappropriation if cash was left undeposited or small valuable inventory was within reach of employees without controls in place. C is wrong. An example of an opportunity to commit fraudulent financial reporting would be if management was dominated by one individual who could override all controls and make journal entries to record fake sales.

57. (A) I is correct. Compensation levels inconsistent with expectations would relate to incentive or perhaps even rationalization to steal. II is wrong. Inadequate segregation of duties provides the opportunity for such theft. Inadequate segregation of duties is neither an incentive nor a pressure but an opportunity. Mandatory vacations can sometimes prevent or detect theft brought about by inadequate segregation of duties.

58. (C) I is correct. If employees are not forced to take vacations, opportunity exists within a company for the misappropriation of assets. Mandatory vacation time would both prevent and detect theft, since less opportunity would exist if the individual already knows that his or her job will be performed by another individual during vacation. Without mandatory vacation policies, the auditor will probably assess inherent risk as high and have to perform additional substantive testing in order to reduce overall audit risk to the level viewed as acceptable. II is correct. If management lacks understanding of the IT used in the company, the auditor would assess inherent risk as high. For both of these situations, additional testing could include use of audit team members with specialized skills, reliance on more physical inspection, testing closer to the end of the fiscal year, and reliance on more sources of information outside of the reporting company.

59. (A) I is correct. Fraudulent financial reporting refers to the purposeful manipulation of a company's financial statements. An auditor should be aware that company officials might be tempted to enter misstatements into the financial records to achieve the desired result. This type of purposeful manipulation of a company's financial statements is sometimes referred to as "cooking the books" and is known on the CPA Exam as fraudulent financial reporting. II is wrong. A company would intentionally manipulate the financial statements to decrease the debt-to-equity ratio, not to increase it.

60. (D) I is wrong. Even if the brainstorming sessions reveal no fraud risk factors, the auditor is still required to inquire regarding management's knowledge of actual or potential fraud. The auditor would inquire how management communicates to employees its views on acceptable business practices and whether there are any particular business segments for which a risk of fraud may be more likely to exist. II is wrong. Even if the brainstorming sessions reveal no fraud risk factors, the auditor is still required to inquire regarding management's programs to mitigate fraud risk.

61. (C) I is correct. In every audit, regardless of the outcome of the brainstorming sessions, revenue recognition is an area considered high risk for fraud. The auditor fears that due to pressures and opportunities, false sales are being recorded or sales are being recorded prior to the earnings process being complete. Since sales have the biggest impact on the income statement, revenue recognition is always an area of concern for an auditor, and analytical procedures would help in this area. The auditor would also test journal entries and inquire about any unusual entries that were made at the end of the year. II is correct. In every audit, regardless of the outcome of the brainstorming sessions, management override of controls is a risk factor for fraudulent financial reporting. The auditor fears that top management could be making adjustments to the financial records that would create misstatements in order to make the company appear more profitable. An auditor would test journal entries for reasonableness and inquire about unusual entries made at year-end.

62. (C) The easiest way for a client to overstate net income is to overstate ending inventory. An overstated ending inventory figure makes cost of goods sold lower than it should be. If cost of goods sold is lower than it should be, gross profit is immediately overstated. In the example that follows, sales are assumed to be $400. Notice how ending inventory being overstated by $20 leads to an overstatement of gross profit. An overstatement of gross profit would then result in an overstatement of net income.

	Correct Amount	Ending Inventory Overstated by $20
Beginning inventory	$0	$0
Purchases	$150	$150
Cost of goods available for sale	$150	$150
Less ending inventory	**$30**	**$50**
Cost of goods sold	**$120**	**$100**
Sales	$400	$400
Less cost of goods sold	**$120**	**$100**
Gross profit	**$280**	**$300**

63. (B) II is correct. Auditors will test journal entries for reasonableness especially where estimates were used in place of actual figures. I is wrong. Making a legal determination of whether fraud occurred would require a legal license, an attorney, and a judge. CPAs do not normally possess such accreditation.

64. (C) I is correct. Analytical procedures are based on the fact that plausible relationships among data may reasonably be expected to exist and continue in the absence of known conditions to the contrary—for example, payroll and payroll tax expense. If payroll increases from Year 1 to Year 2, payroll tax expense should increase also. If payroll increases and payroll tax expense declines, the auditor would want to know why. It could be that the company is behind on the payroll taxes. If so, the auditor would look for a liability on the balance sheet for unpaid payroll taxes. If no such liability exists, the client would be hiding debts. II is correct. Analytical procedures can sometimes substitute for tests of certain balances and transactions. In the case of bonds payable and interest expense, the auditor can perform analytical procedures to compare the expected amount of interest expense to the client's reported figure. In this way, an auditor can sometimes rely on analytical procedures in the evidence-gathering stage of an audit rather than performing a substantive test.

65. (D) I is wrong. Analytical procedures are useful to detect unusual relationships. Analytical procedures consist of evaluations of financial information made by a study of expected relationships among both financial and nonfinancial data. An auditor could rely on a five-year sales trend to estimate sales for Year 6. Plausible relationships among data may reasonably be expected to exist and continue in the absence of known conditions to the contrary. II is wrong. If the auditor knows the number of employees and the average hourly wage, payroll figures can be estimated and then compared to the client-reported figure for reasonableness.

66. (D) I is wrong. Analytical procedures are mandatory in the overall review stage (final moments) of the audit. II is wrong. Analytical procedures are mandatory in the planning stage of the audit. The only stage of the audit that analytical procedures are not likely to be done at all is the internal control stage because the internal control stage does not involve numbers.

67. (D) I is wrong. An auditor of a nonissuer is required to follow Statements on Auditing Standards and should be able to justify any departures. II is wrong. Lack of familiarity with a Statement on Auditing Standards is not a valid reason for departing from its guidance. On rare occasions, auditors may depart from an SAS but must be able to justify the departure.

Chapter 3: Understanding and Testing of Internal Control

68. (D) I is wrong. The control environment does not relate to management's ability to foresee problems. The control environment relates to the tone at the top of an organization. Top management is charged with communicating and demonstrating ethical behavior, and there should be a code of ethics for top management. Those responsible for governance and management of the organization should demonstrate a commitment to ethics by example. II is wrong. The control activities component of internal control refers to safeguarding assets and segregation of duties. Management's ability to foresee problems and take steps to prevent problems describes the risk assessment component of internal control, not the control environment or the control activities.

69. (B) II is correct. Internal controls of all of a reporting entity's operating units and business functions are a primary concern of the entity's management and those charged with governance, such as the audit committee and the board of directors. All of internal control is relevant to the entity, its operating units, and its business functions. I is wrong. While all of internal control is relevant to the entity, not all of a company's internal controls may be relevant to a financial statement audit. The independent auditor is interested in those controls that relate to financial statement assertions.

70. (A) I is correct. An auditor's primary consideration in evaluating controls is whether specific controls affect the account balances on the client's financial statements, since ultimately the auditor must render an opinion on whether the financial statements are fairly presented. II is wrong. Operational controls are relevant to the entity, its operating units, and its business functions. Operational controls are not a primary concern of the independent auditor. The auditor is only concerned with controls that affect the financial statements.

71. (C) III is correct. Control activities relate to segregation of duties and safeguarding assets. I is wrong. The control environment is the tone at the top of the organization charged with communicating and demonstrating ethical behavior. II is wrong. Risk assessment (as one of the five components of internal control) relates to the company's ability to foresee problems and take steps to prevent problems.

72. (A) I is correct. Segregation of duties is tested by making sure that one person is not performing incomparable functions. Testing for segregation of duties does not involve paperwork or even an audit trail. An auditor will observe, inquire, and inspect to test for segregation of duties. II is wrong. This question is about internal control, and, like any other question on internal control, any answer choice to an internal control question that mentions "analytical procedures" is the wrong answer. Analytical procedures are not performed in the internal control stage of the audit. III is wrong. Inspecting and recalculating are substantive tests. The question is about internal control; with internal control questions, an answer choice that involves a substantive test is probably wrong.

73. (C) I is correct. In the internal control stage, an independent auditor searches for control activities to determine whether the opportunities to allow any person to both perpetrate and conceal fraud are minimized. This choice relates to segregation of duties. If duties are properly segregated, the same person would not be able to both steal from the company and cover it up in the accounting records. II is correct. Control activities should be in place to safeguard assets. The auditor observes to make sure safeguards are in place. The auditor would raise his or her assessment of control risk should these safeguards not be found.

74. (B) II is correct. Ongoing monitoring involves assessing the design and operation of controls on a timely basis and taking necessary corrective actions. Such an approach may be followed in reviewing one particular cycle at a time, the payroll cycle or purchasing cycle. I is wrong. Monitoring of internal control is internal, not external, so the annual audit is not considered a monitoring engagement of the client's internal controls.

75. (C) I is correct. The monitoring component of internal control involves assessing the design and operation of controls on a timely basis and taking necessary corrective actions. The auditor looks to see if monitoring of internal control is a priority of the client company because this will impact the auditor's assessment of control risk. II is correct. The monitoring component of internal control involves assessing the design and operation of controls on a timely basis and taking necessary corrective actions. Monitoring is an internal function often performed by the client's internal audit department.

76. (B) II is correct. Control group is not one of the five components of internal control. The control group is involved in internal control in an IT environment but is not a component of overall internal control. III is correct. Control risk is not one of the five components of internal control. Control risk is assessed by the auditor after coming to an understanding of all five components of internal control. The five components of internal control are control environment, risk assessment, control activities, information and communication, monitoring.

77. (D) I is correct. When management is dominated by one individual who is also a shareholder, there may be an opportunity for management to override control procedures. II is correct. Management's emphasis on meeting projected profit goals would significantly influence an entity's control environment when a significant portion of management compensation is represented by stock options, because management would then have a personal interest that might be at odds with accurate financial reporting. III is wrong. If those charged with governance were active in overseeing the entity's financial reporting policies, it would be less likely that management's attitude toward aggressive financial reporting would significantly influence an entity's control environment.

78. (C) Both I and II are correct. As part of gaining an understanding of internal control, the auditor needs to know both the design of the system and whether the system has been put in place. The client could have designed a system of controls, described them in detail to the auditor, but never implemented them. As a next step, the auditor may decide to test controls to see if the controls that have been designed and implemented are functioning as designed to detect and prevent material misstatements.

79. (B) II is correct. As part of gaining an understanding of internal control, the auditor needs to know the design of the client's system and whether the controls have been placed into operation. I is wrong. The auditor is not required to obtain knowledge about the operating effectiveness of controls. Operating effectiveness of the client's internal controls is evaluated later, and only for those controls on which the auditor plans to rely.

80. (A) I is correct. The ultimate purpose of assessing control risk is to determine the nature, extent, and timing of further audit procedures. II is wrong. While recommendations would ordinarily be made if appropriate, the primary reason for the auditor to assess control risk is to evaluate the risk of financial statement misstatement.

81. (A) I is correct. An auditor can assess control risk as low for inventory or any other account balance if the auditor finds an internal control that is relevant and functioning as designed. II is wrong. If control risk is assessed as low, less substantive testing than planned would be performed, not more.

82. **(B)** II is correct. When the auditor chooses the substantive approach, carefully designed substantive tests will substitute for tests of controls to gather sufficient competent evidence to support the opinion. I is wrong. When the auditor chooses the substantive approach, tests of controls are NOT performed. The auditor chooses the substantive approach when internal controls are poor or no time savings would come from testing controls.

83. **(C)** I is correct. An auditor would choose to use the combined approach to further audit procedures if, based on the auditor's assessment of internal control, the auditor thinks the controls are in place. II is correct. An auditor would choose to use the combined approach to further audit procedures if, based on the auditor's assessment of internal control, the auditor thinks the controls are in place and testing controls could reduce substantive procedures.

84. **(B)** II is correct. After gaining and documenting an understanding of the components of internal control, the auditor should make a preliminary assessment of control risk. If the auditor's investigation indicates that internal control is probably weak, the auditor should emphasize substantive testing rather than test of controls. I is wrong. If internal control is considered weak, the amount of substantive testing (performed to decrease detection risk) will be increased, not reduced. Therefore, if the auditor feels that controls are weak, nothing can be gained by testing the controls further. Additional testing of controls is carried out only if the overall amount of audit testing is likely to be reduced.

85. **(C)** I is correct. In developing a questionnaire for a particular system or activity, the auditor considers (1) the general control activities that are applicable, and (2) specific control activities that should be utilized in this system. Then, for each of these anticipated controls, the auditor simply asks a question to see if the activity is actually present in the system. Thus, a "yes" answer means the expected control is included in the design whereas a "no" points up a potential problem. Both the strengths and weaknesses can be easily noted even by an inexperienced auditor. II is correct. Using a flowchart to identify strengths and weaknesses takes a certain amount of experience and expertise compared to a questionnaire, which is easier to use to identify internal control strengths and weaknesses. Because the auditor must gain an understanding of the five components of internal control, documentation is especially important to demonstrate that generally accepted auditing standards have been followed. The auditor can use any of several methods (such as a questionnaire, a flowchart, or a memorandum) to document the understanding of these components that is achieved.

86. **(A)** I is correct. An auditor's flowchart of the accounting system is a diagrammatic representation that shows the auditor's understanding of the system. The auditor must document his or her understanding of the system, and the use of a flowchart is one of several alternatives to comply. II is wrong. While an auditor's flowchart of the accounting system is a diagrammatic representation that shows the auditor's understanding of the system, it does not show the auditor's assessment of control risk. Flowcharting aids the auditor's understanding of the system. The auditor's assessment of control risk is based on the auditor's professional judgment and is not documented graphically.

87. **(B)** Observation of the activity itself is the auditor's best way to test for segregation of duties. For example, the auditor would observe that the same person is not both collecting cash and recording the collection in the accounting records. A is wrong. An auditor can inquire about segregation of duties, but a good auditor would want more than just a response, which is why observation would be a better answer than inquiry regarding segregation of duties. C is wrong. Confirmations are not tests of controls; they are substantive tests. D is wrong. Preparing a flowchart or questionnaire is useful to gain an understanding of the system, but once the auditor decides to test the system, he or she needs to look for control activities that can relate to specific assertions and test those control activities if the auditor seeks to rely on those controls.

88. (A) I is correct. The auditor is interested in discovering the presence of specific control activities that should reduce control risk. For example, if a questionnaire or flowchart shows that an independent party reconciles the cash account each week, that activity (if it is being performed properly) might well reduce the assessment of control risk in this area. II is wrong. Analyzing and confirming are substantive tests, not tests of controls.

89. (A) I is correct. Testing controls is the auditor's best method to determine if controls are functioning as designed in order to rely on that control and possibly reduce substantive testing. II is wrong. The question asks about testing controls. Controls are tested in the internal control stage, whereas account balances are tested using substantive tests in the evidence-gathering stage, a later stage of the audit. The results of the test of controls would be to determine the nature, timing, and extent of substantive tests that, if carefully designed, can estimate account balances and help accomplish specific audit objectives.

90. (D) I is wrong. By "further audit procedures," the auditor chooses either the combined approach or the substantive approach. The auditor doesn't know which approach to choose until the assessment of inherent risk is completed. II is wrong for the same reason. If control risk is assessed as high for a particular account or assertion, the substantive approach would be chosen.

91. (C) I is correct. The external auditor is required to obtain sufficient knowledge of internal control, but he or she is not responsible for establishing, maintaining, and/or monitoring internal control. II is correct. The entity's management is responsible for establishing, maintaining, and monitoring the entity's internal controls, considering whether those controls are operating as intended, and modifying controls as conditions change

92. (C) I is correct. Manual controls are internal controls performed by people and are more suitable when judgment and discretion are required, such as when there are large, unusual, or nonrecurring transactions. II is correct for the same reason.

93. (A) I is correct. When potential misstatements are more difficult to predict, judgment is needed. If judgment is needed, manual controls (humans) are needed rather than computers. Manual controls are internal controls performed by people and are more suitable when judgment and discretion are required, such as when there are large, unusual, or nonrecurring transactions. Such transactions make potential misstatements more difficult to predict. II is wrong. When transactions are high volume and recurring, the auditor expects to find automated controls rather than manual controls.

94. (C) I is correct. Inherent limitations of internal control are limitations that are built in and cannot be entirely prevented. Collusion among employees is an inherent limitation because even when duties are properly segregated, the risk still exists that two or more individuals could combine to steal from the company. Thus, collusion is a built-in, inherent limitation that cannot entirely be prevented. II is correct. Judgments are made by people. Even well-trained employees with experience are not perfect and can make errors in judgment. Thus, errors in judgment are another inherent limitation of internal control.

95. (A) I is correct. Management override of controls is an inherent limitation of internal control. An example of an inherent limitation would be if the CEO is the only employee who can request a check with no purchase order. II is wrong. Incompatible duties are internal control weaknesses but not inherent limitations. An inherent limitation is built in and cannot entirely be prevented. Incompatible duties can be corrected and, therefore, are not inherent limitations.

96. (D) I is correct. In every audit, the audit documentation must contain an indication whether or not the financial statements agree with the accounting records. II is correct. Risk assessment procedures must be performed to assess the risk of material misstatement and to determine whether and to what extent further audit procedures are necessary. Risk assessment procedures are performed during the assessment of inherent risk and control risk. III is wrong. Tests of the operating effectiveness of controls are performed only when the auditor's risk assessment is based on the assumption that controls are operating effectively or when substantive procedures alone are insufficient.

97. (B) When an auditor assesses control risk at the maximum level, the assessment should be documented and the auditor should make decisions to potentially perform more substantive procedures. A is wrong. When the auditor assesses control risk at the maximum, the auditor would perform more substantive tests, not fewer. C is wrong. The documentation would not be more extensive when control risk is assessed at the maximum; the documentation would have to be more detailed when control risk is assessed below the maximum to explain why the assessment is lower than the maximum. The extra documentation would pertain to the controls that were found and how they were tested. D is wrong. Tests of controls are not performed in a GAAS audit unless the auditor believes that control risk is below the maximum.

98. (C) I is correct. Tests of the operating effectiveness of controls are performed only when the auditor's risk assessment is based on the assumption that controls are operating effectively. II is correct. Tests of the operating effectiveness of controls are performed when substantive procedures alone are insufficient, such as when there is no audit trail in an IT environment.

Chapter 4: Audit Documentation, Related-Party Transactions, and Subsequent Events

99. (C) I is correct. The current file is maintained to hold, organize, and document all of the evidence gathered so that the auditor can support this year's audit opinion. II is correct. A working trial balance is meant to resemble the financial statements without footnotes and includes additional columns for reclassifications and adjustments. A working trial balance pertains only to this year's audit, so it belongs in the current file.

100. (A) I is correct. The permanent file is used to store relevant information that would NOT be expected to change significantly from year to year. Such items as contracts, organization charts, chart of account numbers, bond indentures, and the company charter should be kept in the permanent file for reference purposes. II is wrong. The audit plan and management representation letter pertain to the current year audit and should be stored in the current file, not the permanent file.

101. (D) Debt agreements are not expected to change from year to year; therefore, they should be stored in the permanent file. A is wrong. Lead schedules are totals of the client's various accounts that are transferred to the working trial balance. Both the working trial balance and the lead schedule are stored in the current file. B and C are wrong. Attorney's letters and bank statements pertain to the current year audit and should be stored in the current file.

102. (D) III is correct. The lead schedules relate to the current year opinion and are stored in the current file, not the permanent file. Lead schedules are totals of the client's various accounts that are transferred to the working trial balance. IV is correct. The working trial balance relates to the current year opinion and is stored in the current file, not the permanent file. The working trial balance contains all of the client's account balances on a single spreadsheet, with additional columns set up for adjustments and reclassifications. I and II are wrong. Bond indenture agreements and lease agreements are ongoing and would be stored in the permanent file, since they relate to more than just the current year audit. Bond indentures contain the stated rate of interest on the bond, the term of the debt agreement, and any covenants, such as the company being required to maintain a current ratio above 1:1 or the bonds being due immediately.

103. (B) After the documentation completion date, no documents may be deleted. Even "auditor's professional judgment" is not an acceptable excuse for deletion of audit documentation once the documentation completion date has passed. Documents can always be added, but any documents that have been added must be noted. Prior to the documentation completion date, the auditor may change, delete, or discard superseded documents.

104. (C) I is correct. Factors affecting the auditor's judgment regarding audit documentation about the quantity, type, and content of the auditor's working papers for a particular engagement include the type of audit report issued, the condition of the client's records, and the assessed level of control risk. II is correct. Factors affecting the auditor's judgment regarding audit documentation about the quantity, type, and content of the auditor's working papers for a particular engagement include the nature of the engagement and the type of report issued.

105. (A) All audit documentation (working papers) is the property of the independent auditor and is not intended to assist the company's management. B and C are wrong. Audit documentation assists the auditor in both the planning and the supervision of the audit. D is wrong. Audit documentation serves to provide the principal support for the auditor's opinion. Audit working papers can assist the audit team in proving that the audit was conducted in accordance with professional standards.

106. (A) I is correct. The audit procedures directed toward identifying related-party transactions should include considering whether transactions are occurring but are not given proper accounting recognition. II is wrong. If proper disclosures are made, related-party transactions are not required to be recorded on terms equivalent to arm's-length transactions.

The auditor's biggest fear with related-party transactions is not about the terms but rather about disclosure. The auditor fears that the client is going to disguise a related-party transaction and make it appear as if it were arm's-length.

107. (B) II is correct. Related parties sometimes guarantee the debts of affiliates; therefore, reviewing confirmations of loans receivable and payable for indications of loan guarantees would assist the auditor in identifying related party transactions not previously disclosed. I is wrong. Undisclosed related-party transactions tend to be nonrecurring rather than recurring.

108. (C) Both I and II are correct. Material related-party transactions must always be disclosed. Thus, X as the seller and Y as the buyer would have to report the nature of the relationship and provide descriptions and dollar amounts for the transactions.

109. (D) II is correct. A loan with no maturity date would be more likely to suggest a related-party transaction because such terms are not typical. III is correct. A loan made by the client with an extremely low interest rate would be evidence of a related-party loan because again the terms are not typical. I is wrong. Variable rate loans are very common and would not necessarily indicate the existence of a related-party transaction.

110. (D) I is wrong. Selling any asset that has been held for an extended length of time for an amount different from book value is not unusual and would not necessarily indicate the presence of a related-party transaction. II is wrong. If the land had been sold for an amount different from its fair market value or if the payment terms had been unusual, the auditor would probably want to investigate further the possibility of a related-party sale that would need to be disclosed. Remember, the terms don't really matter; the primary auditor concern is that it is disclosed as a related-party transaction.

111. (D) I is incorrect. Comparing the financial statements being reported on with those of the prior period is not a very good source of subsequent event information. II is incorrect. Changes in accounting personnel at any time would probably not result in any subsequent-event financial statement adjustment or disclosure.

112. (C) If the auditor believes that the financial statements need to be revised to reflect a subsequent event and management does not make the revision, the auditor should express a qualified or adverse opinion, since the issue is known to the auditor to be GAAP related. A is wrong. If the auditor believes that the financial statements need to be revised to reflect a subsequent event and management does not make the revision, an unmodified opinion would not be appropriate; the opinion would need to be modified. Simply adding an other-matters paragraph would not be a valid substitute for a qualified or adverse opinion in this case. B is wrong. In this situation, a disclaimer would not be appropriate. Disclaimers are appropriate only in situations where an auditor lacks evidence to support an opinion. This scenario relates to evidence being present, not evidence missing. D is wrong. While a qualified opinion may be appropriate, an unmodified opinion would not be, since the auditor does not agree with management regarding revision of the financial statements. The auditor wants the financial statements revised in order to be fairly presented.

113. (A) I is correct. The auditor has an active responsibility to make continuing inquiries between the date of the financial statements and the date of the auditor's report. II is wrong.

The auditor has no active responsibility to make continuing inquiries between the date of the auditor's report and the date on which the report is submitted. The auditor's active responsibility stops on the date of the auditor's report.

114. (C) The auditor has no active responsibility to make continuing inquiries between the date of the auditor's report and the date on which the report is submitted. The auditor's active responsibility stops on the date of the auditor's report. A and B are wrong. The auditor has an active responsibility to make continuing inquiries between the date of the financial statements and the date of the auditor's report, which is the date on which sufficient appropriate audit evidence has been obtained. D is wrong. The auditor has no active responsibility to make continuing inquiries after the date of the auditor's report.

Chapter 5: Audit Reporting

115. (D) The paragraphs found in a standard unmodified audit report for a nonissuer are introductory paragraph, management's responsibility paragraph, auditor's responsibility paragraph, and opinion paragraph. There is no more "scope" paragraph.

116. (B) There are four paragraphs in a standard unmodified audit report: introductory paragraph, management's responsibility paragraph, auditor's responsibility paragraph, and opinion paragraph.

117. (D) There are four paragraphs in a standard unmodified audit report and should appear in this order: introductory paragraph, management's responsibility paragraph, auditor's responsibility paragraph, and opinion paragraph There is no more "scope" paragraph in an audit report.

118. (D) The audit report does not state that the auditor evaluated the overall internal control. The correct statement is "In making those risk assessments, the auditor considers internal control relevant to the entity's preparation and fair presentation of the financial statements in order to design audit procedures that are appropriate in the circumstances, but not for the purpose of expressing an opinion on the effectiveness of the entity's internal control."

119. (B) II is correct. In the opinion paragraph, the auditor uses the terms *present fairly* and *US GAAP*. I is wrong. It is in the auditor's responsibility paragraph, not the opinion paragraph, that the auditor mentions assessing the accounting principles and evaluating significant accounting estimates used by the reporting entity.

120. (C) I is correct. The auditor's standard report implies that the auditor is satisfied that the comparability of financial statements between periods has not been materially affected by changes in accounting principles. II is correct. The auditor's standard report implies that the auditor is satisfied that the comparability of financial statements between periods has not been materially affected by changes in accounting principles and that such principles have been applied consistently between or among periods. Since the auditor has gathered sufficient evidence about consistency, no reference need be made in the report.

121. (C) I is correct. An emphasis-of-matter paragraph is included in the auditor's report when required by GAAS. The emphasis-of-matter paragraph is required when the auditor concludes that there is substantial doubt about an entity's ability to continue as a going concern or when there is a justified change in accounting principles that has a material effect on the entity's financial statements. II is correct. An emphasis-of-matter paragraph is included in the auditor's report at the auditor's discretion anytime the auditor wants to emphasize a matter, possibly regarding uncertainty or related-party transactions.

122. (B) II is correct. An inclusion of an emphasis-of-matter paragraph in the auditor's report does not affect the auditor's opinion. The auditor's opinion is still unmodified. I is wrong. An inclusion of an emphasis-of-matter paragraph in the auditor's report is used when referring to a matter that is appropriately presented in the financial statements.

123. (D) I is wrong. The emphasis-of-matter paragraph should be placed after the opinion paragraph. The auditor can always emphasize a matter in connection with a set of financial statements by adding a paragraph after the opinion paragraph. This paragraph allows the auditor to draw the reader's attention to any specific information that might be deemed essential. II is wrong. The emphasis paragraph should state that the auditor's opinion is not modified.

124. (C) I is correct. An other-matters paragraph is required when the auditor's report needs to be restricted. The restriction is placed in an other-matters paragraph immediately following any emphasis paragraph (after the opinion). II is correct. The auditor is always permitted to add an other-matters paragraph. Unlike the emphasis-of-matter paragraph, the other-matters paragraph is used to describe something that is not already presented or disclosed in the financial statements and that is relevant to the user's understanding of the audit.

125. (A) II and III are correct. Other-matters paragraphs refer to matters other than those presented or disclosed in the financial statements that are relevant to the user's understanding of the auditor's responsibilities. I is wrong. Other-matters paragraphs are relevant to the user's understanding of the audit, not to the user's understanding of the financial statements. The other-matters paragraph generally describes matters other than those presented or disclosed in the financial statements.

126. (A) I is correct. An auditor would express an unmodified opinion with an emphasis-of-matter paragraph added to the auditor's report for a justified change in accounting principle. The emphasis-of-matter paragraph should be placed after the opinion paragraph. II is wrong. A material weakness must be reported to management and those charged with governance, but it would not be disclosed in an emphasis-of-matter paragraph added to an otherwise unmodified opinion.

127. (C) I is correct. The preparation and fair presentation of the financial statements requires identification of the applicable financial reporting framework. II is correct. The preparation and fair presentation of the financial statements also requires an adequate description of the framework in the financial statements. While US GAAP is the likely framework, other frameworks are acceptable, such as IFRS.

128. (D) I is wrong. Twelve months is not mentioned in the going concern paragraph, nor is any other amount of time. II is wrong. Reasonable period of time is not expressed in the emphasis-of-matter paragraph either. The two required phrases in an emphasis-of-matter paragraph relating to going concern are "reasonable doubt" and "going concern."

129. (D) An auditor would generally issue an unmodified audit opinion without an emphasis-of-matter paragraph or other-matters paragraph when the auditor decides to make reference to the audit of a component auditor as a basis, in part, for the auditor's opinion. The auditor would modify his or her report but would not add a paragraph. The reference to the other auditor would be in the auditor's responsibility paragraph and opinion paragraph.

130. (B) II is correct. The introductory paragraph does not change whether the auditor divides responsibility or assumes responsibility for the component auditor. I is wrong. In a division of responsibility, the group auditor would specify the amount of assets and revenues audited by the other firm (magnitude). This reference would be made in the auditor's responsibility paragraph.

131. (C) I is correct. The auditor's report should include a reference to the country of origin of the auditing standards that the auditor followed in performing the audit. If US GAAS was followed in conducting the audit, the report should so indicate by mentioning the country as well as the standards. II is correct. The auditor's report should include a reference to the country of origin of the accounting principles used to prepare the financial statements. If US GAAP was used to prepare the financial statements, the report should mention the country as well as the standards.

132. (C) I is correct. Change in useful life of an asset is a change in estimate, handled prospectively. Since the change in useful life is not considered a change in accounting principle, there is no consistency issue, so an unmodified opinion is proper. II is correct. Change in depreciation method is considered a change in principle, inseparable from a change in estimate, and is handled prospectively as a change in estimate. Since it is not considered a change in principle, consistency is not an issue; therefore, an unmodified opinion is proper.

133. (D) Neither I nor II is correct. The principal may decide that the problem encountered by the other auditor is material to the consolidated statements. If that decision is made, a qualified opinion should be rendered by the principal. However, a problem that was material to a portion of the statements may not necessarily be material to the consolidated statements as a whole. The principal is not required to issue a qualified opinion. The auditor's professional judgment would be the final determinate.

134. (B) II is correct. If the previous accounting principle was NOT in conformity with GAAP, the emphasis-of-matter paragraph would still be required. I is wrong. When a client changes an accounting principle that has a material effect on the financial statements but the auditor concurs with the change, an emphasis-of-matter paragraph would be required, but it would not need to go before the opinion. Rather, it would likely be placed after the opinion, since the opinion is still unmodified.

135. (A) I is correct. When an auditor qualifies an opinion because of a scope limitation, the wording in the opinion paragraph should indicate that the qualification pertains to the possible impact on the financial statements. II is wrong. When an auditor qualifies an opinion because of a scope limitation, the wording in the opinion paragraph should indicate that the qualification pertains to the scope limitation itself. The scope limitation is described in an additional paragraph, known as the basis for qualified opinion paragraph.

136. (A) I is correct. A change in depreciation method is considered a change in accounting estimate and is accounted for prospectively. It does not affect comparability, so consistency would not be addressed in the report. II is wrong. Consistency would be a concern and need to be expressed with the use of an emphasis-of-matter paragraph when the previous accounting principle was not GAAP because a change in accounting principle affects comparability.

137. (B) If a company issues financial statements that purport to present financial position and results of operations but omit the related statement of cash flows, the auditor will normally conclude that the omission requires qualification of the opinion. A and C are wrong. The statement of cash flows is a required financial statement. Omitting the statement of cash flows would be an example of financial statements that are less than "fairly presented"; therefore, an unmodified opinion would not be allowed even with an emphasis paragraph. D is wrong. Disclaimers of opinion are not rendered when the financial statements are less than "fairly presented." Disclaimers are only rendered when evidence to support an opinion is lacking.

138. (B) II is correct. The opinion paragraph in an adverse opinion should state that, in the auditor's opinion, because of the significance of the matters described in the basis for adverse opinion paragraph, the financial statements are not presented fairly. I is wrong. When an auditor expresses an adverse opinion, the opinion paragraph should not include the substantive reasons for the financial statements being misleading. The rationale for the adverse opinion should be found in an additional paragraph called the basis for adverse opinion paragraph.

139. (C) I is correct. Inadequate disclosure is a GAAP problem. GAAP problems result in audit opinions that are qualified or adverse if not unmodified. II is correct. A change in accounting principle is a GAAP issue also resulting in an audit opinion that is qualified or adverse if not unmodified. Disclaimer is only for GAAS-related issues, and the lack of evidence would have to be rather extreme.

140. (D) If an auditor finds misstatements that are material but not pervasive, a qualified opinion is expressed. A is wrong. If an auditor finds misstatements that are material, the auditor would likely not issue an unmodified (clean) opinion but rather a qualified opinion. B is wrong. For an adverse opinion to be expressed, the misstatements would likely be pervasive (widespread) as well as material. C is wrong. A disclaimer would not be appropriate for a material misstatement. Disclaimers are issued for a lack of evidence.

141. (C) When an auditor expresses a qualified opinion due to a material misstatement of the financial statements, the auditor's responsibility paragraph should be amended to state that the auditor believes that the audit evidence obtained is sufficient and appropriate to provide a basis for the auditor's qualified opinion.

142. (B) II is correct. Consistent application of accounting principles is implied in the auditor's report. The auditor makes no mention of consistency unless there is an inconsistency in application of accounting principles. I is wrong. Under US generally accepted auditing standards, the auditor explicitly states in the auditor's responsibility paragraph of the opinion: "We believe that the audit evidence we have obtained is sufficient and appropriate to provide a basis for our audit opinion."

143. (D) II and III are correct. If the auditor is unable to form an opinion on a new client's opening inventory balances, the auditor will issue an opinion on the closing balance sheet only and will issue a disclaimer of opinion on both the income statement and the statement of cash flows. I is wrong. If the auditor is unable to form an opinion on a new client's opening inventory balances, the auditor will issue an opinion on the closing balance sheet only. The auditor will then issue a disclaimer of opinion on the income statement, the statement of retained earnings, and the statement of cash flows.

144. (D) I is wrong. When an auditor expresses an adverse opinion or disclaimer on a complete set of financial statements, the auditor's report should not also include an unmodified opinion on a single financial statement. II is wrong. When an auditor expresses an adverse opinion or disclaimer on a complete set of financial statements, the auditor's report should not also include an unmodified opinion on property, plant, and equipment or any other specific element, account, or item of a financial statement. Issuing an unmodified opinion in these circumstances would contradict the adverse opinion or the disclaimer of opinion on the financial statements taken as a whole.

Chapter 6: Reviews and Compilations

145. (D) SSARS applies to compilations and reviews of non-publicly traded companies. A and B are wrong. SSARS applies to both compilations and reviews. C is wrong. Public company reviews are governed by SAS.

146. (C) I is correct. Gathering evidence regarding a client's ability to continue as a going concern is not considered part of a review engagement. II is correct. Inquiries of the entity's outside legal counsel are not performed in a review. In a review, inquiries tend to be internal; the auditor inquires within the organization, not to outside parties.

147. (A) I is correct. An accountant is not required to assess control risk as part of a review engagement. Assessment of control risk would be appropriate for an audit engagement. II is wrong. Inquiring of management is the primary source of review evidence, so inquiring to management regarding subsequent events is an appropriate review procedure.

148. (D) I is wrong. Analytical procedures are mandatory in a review engagement (and audit) but are not likely to be performed in a compilation. II is wrong. Inquiries are mandatory in a review engagement and audit but are not likely to be performed in a compilation. A compilation merely involves taking management information, creating financial statements, and issuing a compilation report. No assurance is given that the financial statements are in conformity with the reporting framework.

149. (B) II is correct. The accountant may decline to issue a compilation report provided that each page of the financial statements is clearly marked to restrict its use and a written engagement letter is used to document the understanding with the client. I is wrong.

Since inquiries are NOT required in a compilation, representation letters are not needed with a compilation engagement.

150. (D) I is wrong. If the accountant concludes that there is reasonable justification to change the engagement, the accountant's report should NOT include reference to the original engagement. II is wrong. If the accountant concludes that there is reasonable justification to change the engagement, the accountant's report should NOT include reference to any procedures that may have been performed or to the scope limitation that resulted in the changed engagement.

151. (B) An accountant with an immaterial direct financial interest in a client is no longer independent with respect to that client. The accountant is precluded from issuing a review report on the financial statements of an entity with respect to which he or she is not independent. If the accountant is not independent, he or she may issue a compilation report provided the accountant complies with the compilation standards. A is wrong. If requested to perform a review engagement for a nonissuer in which an accountant has an immaterial direct financial interest, a review cannot be performed but a compilation may be performed provided lack of independence is disclosed. C is wrong. If requested to perform a review engagement for a nonissuer in which an accountant has an immaterial direct financial interest, a review cannot be performed; however, the accountant can still be associated with the financial statements and a compilation may be performed. D is wrong. If requested to perform a review engagement for a nonissuer in which an accountant has an immaterial direct financial interest, the accountant is not independent.

152. (D) A review provides limited assurance that there are no material modifications that should be made to the financial statements in order for them to be in conformity with generally accepted accounting principles, whereas a compilation provides no assurance. A is wrong. A compilation does not provide limited assurance that the CPA followed SSARS, nor does a compilation provide limited assurance that the client followed GAAP. A compilation provides no assurance. B and C are wrong. A compilation does not provide negative or limited assurance; a compilation provides no assurance.

153. (D) I is wrong. A compilation does not test for reasonableness of the financial statements. A compilation provides no assurance and includes no testing. A compilation often involves just reading the financial statements to consider whether they are free of obvious mistakes in the application of accounting principles. II is wrong. A review does not test for reasonableness of the financial statements. A review provides limited assurance that no material modifications need to be made to the financial statements. In a review, limited assurance is based on inquiry and analytical procedures.

154. (B) An accountant who is not independent with respect to an entity may compile financial statements for such an entity and issue a report. The last paragraph of the report should disclose this lack of independence. The accountant is permitted, but not required, to disclose the reasons for the lack of independence. A is wrong. If independence is compromised, a CPA cannot express limited assurance on the financial statements because a CPA must be independent to perform such an engagement (review). C is wrong. The CPA does not have to be independent of the reporting entity when performing a compilation. If the CPA is not independent, the CPA would disclose the lack of independence in the compilation report and thus there would be no need to withdraw from the engagement.

155. (A) An unmodified review report under Statements on Standards for Accounting and Review Services (SSARS) for a nonissuer contains four paragraphs: (1) introductory paragraph, (2) management responsibility paragraph, (3) CPA's responsibility paragraph, and (4) limited assurance paragraph.

156. (D) The second paragraph of the four paragraphs found in the standard review report for a nonissuer is known as the management responsibility paragraph. An unmodified review report under Statements on Standards for Accounting and Review Services (SSARS) for a nonissuer contains four paragraphs in the following order: (1) introductory paragraph, (2) management responsibility paragraph, (3) CPA's responsibility paragraph, and (4) limited assurance paragraph.

157. (C) I is correct. As part of a review for a nonissuer, an engagement letter is mandatory and needs to be signed by the client to minimize the risk of a misunderstanding regarding the responsibilities of the CPA and management. II is correct. As part of a review engagement for a nonissuer, a management representation letter is required because a review involves inquiries from the CPA that management normally responds to orally. The CPA needs to turn that oral evidence into written evidence by writing down management's responses and presenting them to management for signature as part of the final review evidence.

158. (A) I is correct. As part of a compilation for a nonissuer, an engagement letter is mandatory. II is wrong. A management representation letter is not required as part of a compilation engagement for a nonissuer, since no inquiries are made in a compilation that involve written management responses.

159. (C) A compilation is merely the production of financial statements from information given to the CPA by the client. No testing, not even analytical procedures, are performed in a compilation engagement. A compilation is often limited to reading the financial statements to consider whether they are free of obvious mistakes in the application of accounting principles. Therefore, A, B, and D are wrong.

160. (A) A standard compilation report contains three paragraphs: (1) introductory paragraph, (2) management responsibility paragraph, and (3) CPA's responsibility paragraph. Additional paragraphs may be needed if the CPA is not independent or if financial statement disclosures are purposely being omitted.

161. (D) A compilation report presented without footnotes by a CPA who is not independent can be performed provided the report discloses both the lack of independence and the fact that the footnotes are missing. This would be accomplished by adding two paragraphs to the compilation report. The report would contain an additional paragraph for the lack of independence and another additional paragraph to mention the fact that required footnotes are missing. The report would have five paragraphs rather than three. A is wrong. Lack of independence is not a factor for a compilation as long as it's disclosed in a separate paragraph. B is wrong. A compilation can be performed even if the disclosures are omitted provided the lack of disclosure is mentioned in a separate paragraph. C is wrong. In a compilation in which the CPA lacks independence, the reason for lack of independence is not generally provided. If one reason for lack of independence is mentioned, then all instances of lack of independence must be disclosed.

162. (C) A standard compilation report contains three paragraphs: (1) introductory paragraph, (2) management responsibility paragraph, and (3) CPA's responsibility paragraph. Additional paragraphs may be needed if the CPA is not independent or if financial statement disclosures are purposely being omitted. An unmodified review report under Statements on Standards for Accounting and Review Services (SSARS) for a nonissuer contains four paragraphs in the following order: (1) introductory paragraph, (2) management responsibility paragraph, (3) CPA's responsibility paragraph, and (4) limited assurance paragraph.

163. (C) II is correct. An engagement letter is required in a review and compilation so that there is no misunderstanding with the client as to the CPA's responsibilities. Without a signed engagement letter, there is a risk that the client thinks the engagement is an audit rather than a review, or a review rather than a compilation. I is wrong. Ordinarily, a review or compilation is suitable for general use and needs no restriction. Each page of the client's financial statements should be stamped, "see CPA's compilation report" or "see CPA's review report." III is wrong. While analytical procedures and inquiries are performed as part of a review engagement, they are not performed as part of a compilation engagement.

164. (A) I is correct. A review of a nonpublic entity requires independence, and the CPA provides limited assurance, not an opinion, that no material modifications need be made to the financial statements for them to be in accordance with the framework. II is wrong. The CPA need not be independent when performing a compilation. No procedures are performed in a compilation, so no assurance is provided. A compilation is often limited to reading the financial statements to consider whether they are free of obvious mistakes in the application of accounting principles. Whether or not the financial statements being reported on contained footnotes is irrelevant.

165. (D) I is wrong. A review of a nonpublic entity requires independence, and the CPA provides limited assurance that no material modifications need be made to the financial statements for them to be in accordance with the framework. II is wrong. The CPA need NOT be independent when performing a compilation. No procedures are performed, so no assurance is provided. A compilation is often limited to reading the financial statements to consider whether they are free of obvious mistakes in the application of accounting principles.

Chapter 7: Reporting on Special Purpose Frameworks and Other Reporting Issues

166. (D) I is correct. A special purpose framework is a financial basis of accounting other than GAAP that includes cash-basis financial reporting. II is correct. A special purpose framework is a financial basis of accounting other than GAAP that includes income tax basis financial reporting. III is correct. Reporting to comply with regulatory requirements fits a special purpose framework that deviates from traditional GAAP reporting.

167. (C) I is correct. An auditor's report on financial statements prepared using the income tax basis will contain an emphasis-of-matter paragraph alerting the reader to a framework different from GAAP. II is correct. An auditor's report on the cash-basis financial statements will contain an emphasis-of-matter paragraph alerting the reader to a framework different from GAAP.

168. (A) I is correct. A report on special purpose framework financial statements should include an emphasis-of-matter paragraph stating the basis, referring to the footnote that describes it, and indicating that it is a non-GAAP basis. II is wrong. A report on special purpose framework financial statements does not include an evaluation of the usefulness of the basis of accounting.

169. (B) I, II, and III are correct. A report on special purpose framework financial statements prepared on the income tax basis should include an emphasis-of-matter paragraph that (1) states the basis of accounting used, (2) refers to the footnote that describes the income tax basis, and (3) indicates that it is a non-GAAP basis.

170. (A) I is correct. A report on a client's compliance with a regulatory requirement, assuming the report is prepared based on a financial statement audit of the complete financial statements, would contain restricted use language. II is wrong. A report on financial statements prepared in conformity with a special purpose framework (such as the cash basis) does not require a restriction on the use of the report.

171. (D) I and II are wrong. Neither the cash basis nor income tax basis reporting requires the auditor to restrict the use of the report. Therefore, the auditor's report will NOT contain a restricted use paragraph (i.e., an other-matters paragraph).

172. (C) I is correct. An auditor's report on special purpose financial statements prepared in accordance with a regulatory basis not intended for general use should include an emphasis-of-matter paragraph that indicates that the financial statements are prepared in accordance with the applicable special purpose framework. II is correct. An auditor's report on special purpose financial statements prepared in accordance with a regulatory basis not intended for general use should include an other-matters paragraph that restricts the use of the auditor's report to those within the entity, the parties to the contract or agreement, or the regulatory agencies to which the entity is subject.

173. (D) I is wrong. A dual opinion on special purpose framework and GAAP would not be required if the financial statements were prepared on the income tax basis. II is wrong. A dual opinion on special purpose framework and GAAP would not be required if the financial statements were prepared on the cash basis. A dual opinion would apply only to financial statements prepared on a regulatory basis that are intended for general use. Then and only then would the auditor have to give an opinion on both conformity with GAAP and also whether the statements present fairly in accordance with the special purpose framework designed by the regulatory agency.

174. (D) An audit of a single financial statement is permitted under US GAAS. An audit of a single financial statement can be performed as a separate audit or in conjunction with an audit of the complete set of financial statements. An audit of a single financial statement is permitted under US GAAS, as it merely involves special considerations in the application of the standards. A is wrong. An audit of a single financial statement can be performed as a separate audit or in conjunction with an audit of the complete set of financial statements. B is wrong. Compliance with this request would not violate any ethical standards of the profession. C is wrong. The auditor must be independent to perform an audit.

175. (C) I is correct. In auditing a single financial statement, the auditor should perform procedures, as necessary, on interrelated items. II is correct. The auditor can perform the audit as either a separate engagement or in conjunction with an audit of the complete set of financial statements.

176. (B) II is correct. The auditor, when auditing a single financial statement, is required to understand the intended users of the financial statement. I is wrong. When auditing a single financial statement and not a complete set, the auditor should determine materiality for the single financial statement.

177. (A) I is correct. An auditor who expresses an adverse opinion but still wishes to express an unmodified opinion on a specific element of those financial statements may do so if the specific element does not constitute a major portion of the entity's complete set of financial statements or the specific element is not based on net income or stockholders' equity. II is wrong. The report on the specific element would have to be a separate report and cannot accompany the auditor's report on the complete set of financial statements.

178. (C) I is correct. An auditor's report would be designated a report on compliance when it is issued in connection with compliance with aspects of regulatory requirements related to audited financial statements. II is correct. It should be noted that a report on compliance in connection with audited financial statements provides negative assurance on compliance.

179. (D) I is wrong. To issue a report on compliance, the auditor must have audited the client's financial statements. II is wrong. To issue a report on compliance, the auditor may only issue negative assurance on compliance.

180. (D) I is wrong. If the auditor finds one or more instances of noncompliance, the report on compliance should describe the noncompliance rather than express negative assurance. II is wrong. If an adverse opinion or disclaimer is expressed on the financial statements, a report on compliance can be issued only when there are material instances of noncompliance. In this case, negative assurance would not be appropriate.

181. (B) II is correct. The report, if separate, would contain a restricted use paragraph. I is wrong. The auditor's report on compliance with a regulatory requirement can be separate or combined as an other-matters paragraph in the auditor's report on the financial statements.

182. (C) I is correct. The auditor's report on compliance should contain a restriction on the use of the report if the report is issued separately. II is correct. The auditor's report on compliance should include a restriction on the use of the report as an other-matters paragraph if the report on compliance is not issued separately but included as part of an auditor's report on complete financial statements.

183. (C) Both I and II are correct. The auditor's report on compliance should contain negative assurance regarding compliance if no instances of noncompliance are found, whether the report was combined or separate.

184. (B) II is correct. The auditor's report on compliance issued as a separate report should contain a statement that the audit was not directed primarily toward obtaining knowledge regarding compliance. In addition, a paragraph that restricts the use of the auditor's report to management, those charged with governance, others within the organization, the regulatory agencies, or the other parties to the contract should be included in a separate report on compliance. I is wrong. The auditor's report on compliance issued as a separate report should be dated the same as the auditor's report on the complete financial statements.

185. (B) The auditor's standard report on compliance issued separately should contain three paragraphs: introductory paragraph, negative assurance paragraph, and restricted use paragraph.

186. (C) I is correct. A special purpose framework is a financial basis of accounting other than GAAP that includes cash basis. Reporting to comply with cash basis fits a special purpose that deviates from traditional GAAP reporting. II is correct. A special purpose framework is a financial basis of accounting other than GAAP that includes reporting to comply with regulatory requirements.

187. (B) II is correct. Negative assurance is provided in reports on compliance with aspects of contractual agreements and reports on regulatory requirements related to audited financial statements. Saying, "We are not aware of any instances of noncompliance" is considered giving negative assurance. I is wrong. Cash basis, tax basis, and other non-GAAP reports provide positive rather than negative assurance. The emphasis-of-matter paragraph in the report indicates that the financial statements (elements, accounts, items) were prepared in accordance with the applicable special purpose framework (positive assurance).

188. (A) If there are both emphasis-of-matter and other-matters paragraphs in an auditor's report, the opinion paragraph would be followed by the emphasis-of-matter paragraph, which would be followed by the other-matters paragraph.

189. (C) I is correct. An auditor may report on summary financial statements that are derived from complete financial statements if the auditor indicates in the report whether the information in the summary financial statements is fairly stated in all material respects in relation to the complete financial statements from which it has been derived. II is correct. An auditor may report on summary financial statements that are derived from complete financial statements if the auditor indicates in the report the date of the auditor's report and the type of opinion expressed on the complete financial statements.

190. (C) I is correct. The auditor should not accept an engagement to report on compliance with a regulatory requirement unless the auditor also is engaged to audit the complete financial statements. II is correct for the same reason. The auditor needs to have been engaged to audit the complete financial statements if the auditor is to prepare a report on compliance or a report on summary financial statements.

191. (B) II is correct. The CPA must follow PCAOB standards when associated with interim reporting required by the SEC. When an entity is required by the SEC to file a quarterly report, the SEC also requires that an independent accountant perform a review. The review also follows PCAOB standards. I is wrong. When an entity is required by the SEC to file a quarterly report, the SEC also requires that an independent accountant perform a review, not an audit, of the interim financial information.

192. (C) I is correct. As part of a review, the accountant is required to inquire of management about suspected fraud. Internal inquiry is a large part of a review. II is correct. As part of a review, the accountant is required to inquire of management about allegations of fraud.

193. (D) I is correct. An accountant's knowledge of an entity's business and its internal control influences the inquiries made. II is correct. An accountant's knowledge of an entity's business and its internal control influences the analytical procedures performed. III is wrong. An interim review does not involve observation of inventory. A review is primarily inquiry and analytical procedures, not evidence gathering.

194. (B) II is correct. A review of the interim financial information of a publicly held company is conducted in accordance with Public Company Accounting Oversight Board (PCAOB) standards. I is wrong. Statements on Standards for Accounting and Review Services (SSARS) apply to reviews of the financial statements of nonissuers.

195. (B) II is correct. As part of a review of interim financial information, the accountant is required to inquire of management about their knowledge of fraud, suspected fraud, or allegations of fraud. I is wrong. A review of interim financial information is not designed to provide information regarding an entity's ability to continue as a going concern.

196. (A) I is correct. As part of a review, the accountant is required to compare disaggregated revenue data for the current interim period with that of comparable prior periods. Disaggregated data refers to data that are broken out from a total. An example of disaggregated data would include revenue by month and revenue by product line. Comparing disaggregated data of current and prior periods is an example of analytical procedures. II is incorrect. Benchmarking, or comparing amounts to industry standards, is an optional analytical procedure for a review but is not required.

197. (A) I is correct. Internal inquiries, that is, inquiries of management, are required in a review of interim financial information of an issuer. II is wrong. External inquiries are permitted but not required.

198. (D) I is correct. Inquiry regarding compliance with GAAP or another framework is required in a review of interim financial statements. II is correct. A written understanding in the form of a signed engagement letter is mandatory in a review of interim financial statements so that there is no misunderstanding regarding the responsibility being assumed by the CPA. In a review, a CPA doesn't want management to mistakenly think an audit is being performed. III is correct. A representation letter signed by management is required in a review of interim financial statements because a review consists primarily of inquiry (oral questions), and responses to inquiry are often oral responses. At the conclusion of the interim review, the CPA asks management to sign the rep letter. By having management sign the rep letter, the CPA is making sure that management understood the oral inquiry and that management still believe in their oral responses to the inquiry.

199. (A) I is correct. Identified risks of material misstatement due to fraud help the accountant to identify the types of material misstatements that may occur in the interim financial information and to consider the likelihood of their occurrence. II is wrong. Scope limitations relate to problems in performing an engagement, but since they were overcome, they would bear little relationship to procedures performed in a review.

200. **(C)** I is correct. A comfort letter is a letter for an underwriter from an auditor and contains a restriction of use. II is correct. In a comfort letter, the CPA gives negative assurance regarding unaudited information and positive assurance regarding audited information.

Chapter 8: Attestation Engagements Other than Audits of Historic Financial Information

201. **(D)** I is correct. In an attestation, sufficient evidence should be obtained to provide a reasonable basis for the conclusion that is expressed in the report. An attestation is a very high level of service and requires both independence and evidence gathering to support the opinion being rendered. II is correct. In an attestation, the work needs to be planned and supervised. III is wrong. A sufficient understanding of internal control is not required to be obtained in an attestation engagement involving an examination of forward-looking financial statements. *Exam hint:* If the question asks about attestation, ask yourself what the answer would be if the question were about an audit (which is a type of attestation). Usually the answer would be the same, unless the answer had something to do with internal control. An audit looks backward at historic financial information, whereas other attestations may look forward. Another difference between an attestation and an audit is that an audit requires internal control work while other attestations often do not.

202. **(D)** I, II, and III are correct. Trust services are assurance and advisory services used to address the risks and opportunities of information technology. Security, availability, processing integrity, online privacy, and confidentiality are the five essential principles that guide a trust engagement.

203. **(C)** Both I and II are correct. Trust services, whether WebTrust or SysTrust, follow attestation standards, since the CPA needs to be independent and an opinion will be rendered.

204. **(B)** A WebTrust engagement is an attestation engagement designed to measure transaction integrity, information protection, and disclosure of business practices. When an unmodified report is issued, the client may add the CPA WebTrust Seal to its website, indicating that its site is a reasonably safe and private place for e-commerce.

205. **(B)** II is correct. Statements on Standards for Attestation Engagements (SSAE) do not apply to tax preparation. I is wrong. SSAE apply to pro forma financial statements.

206. **(D)** I is wrong. SSAE apply to forecasts, or forward-looking financial statements that are intended for general use. II is wrong. SSAE apply to projections, or forward-looking financial statements that are NOT intended for general use. Projections will contain a restriction on use, but the same standards apply. Other engagements for which SSAE apply include separate engagements regarding internal control, pro forma, compliance agreements, and agreed-upon procedures.

207. **(D)** I is correct. SSAE do not apply to audits of nonissuers; Statements on Auditing Standards (SAS) would apply. II is correct. SSAE do not apply to compilations because Statements on Standards for Accounting and Review Services (SSARS) apply to compilations. III is correct. SSAE do not apply to reviews of nonissuers; rather, SSARS apply to reviews of nonissuers.

208. (D) I is wrong. Agreed-upon procedures engagements follow Statements on Standards for Attestation Engagements. There is no such thing as Statements on Standards for Agreed-Upon Procedures. II is wrong. The CPA must be independent to perform agreed-upon procedures. In an agreed-upon procedures engagement, parties must agree to the procedures performed by the CPA, unlike an audit, where the auditor comes in with his or her own audit plan.

209. (A) I is correct. Use of the report is restricted to the specified parties. II is wrong. In an agreed-upon procedures engagement, the client is responsible for the subject matter and its adequacy. The items being reported on must be measurable and result in reasonably consistent findings. Furthermore, evidence to support the report should be expected to exist. The parties need to agree to the procedures performed by the CPA.

210. (B) II is correct. The agreed-upon procedures report is limited in distribution. I is wrong. In an agreed-upon procedures engagement, the CPA lists the procedures and the findings but does not provide any assurance.

211. (B) II is correct. The CPA must be independent when applying agreed-upon procedures even though no assurance is provided. The report describes the procedures and the CPA's findings without providing any assurance. I is wrong. A review of a nonpublic entity requires independence, and the CPA provides limited assurance that no material modifications need be made to the financial statements for them to be in accordance with the framework.

212. (C) I is correct. A review of a nonpublic entity requires independence, but the CPA expresses no opinion. Instead, the CPA provides limited assurance that no material modifications need be made to the financial statements for them to be in accordance with the framework. Note that in a review engagement, no opinion is expressed, and limited assurance is provided. II is correct. The CPA must be independent when applying agreed-upon procedures even though no opinion is provided. The report describes the procedures and the CPA's findings without providing any assurance.

213. (B) II is correct. Examination of a financial forecast includes evaluating—and giving an opinion after evaluating—the preparation of a financial forecast and the support underlying management's assumptions, similar to an audit. I is wrong. Compiling involves a lower level of service with regard to the financial forecast. Compiling the forecast would not involve evaluating or gathering evidence to support the forecast.

214. (A) I is correct. Whenever an accountant reports on prospective financial statements, the report should include a caveat that prospective results may not be achieved. II is wrong. A review of a forecast or projection is not an appropriate level of service for a forecast or projection. Review engagements look backward at historical financial information. Forecasts and projections are forward looking. *Exam hint:* Do not use the term *review* or *audit* unless the financial information is historic.

215. (A) I is correct. Compilations of projections follow Statements on Standards for Attestation Engagements (SSAE). II is wrong. Compilations of historical financial statements follow Statements on Standards for Accounting and Review Services (SARS).

216. (C) I is correct. Since a written assertion has not been provided, when reporting directly on subject matter, the report should be restricted to specified parties. II is correct. Use of the accountant's report should be restricted to specified parties when reporting on an agreed-upon procedures engagement.

217. (B) II is correct. In an attestation engagement where the CPA examines and reports directly on subject matter, the report indicates what the subject matter was that the CPA examined. A report directly on the subject matter would say something like, "We have examined the accompanying schedule, the profit-sharing plan, for the purposes of determining if management is contributing sufficiently to the plan." Since the CPA is reporting directly on the subject matter, the CPA mentions the subject matter, that is, the accompanying schedule. I is wrong. In an attestation engagement where the CPA examines and reports directly on subject matter, the report indicates what the subject matter was that the CPA examined. The CPA would not mention any assertion made by management unless the CPA was hired to report on management's assertion. If the CPA was hired to report on management's assertion, the report might then say, "We have examined management's assertion that they have contributed the appropriate amount into the profit-sharing plan."

218. (B) II is correct. Negative assurance may be expressed when an accountant reports on the results of performing a review of management's assertion. Review engagements lead to the CPA's giving negative assurance. Negative assurance includes using phrases such as "Nothing came to our attention" or "We are not aware." Even in a review of historical financial statements, negative language is used, but in that one instance it is called limited assurance rather than negative assurance. I is wrong. Negative assurance is not provided in a compilation of prospective financial statements; no assurance is provided in a compilation of prospective financial statements.

219. (A) I is correct. When performing an attestation engagement related to a client's prospective financial statements, the accountant should ensure that the client discloses all significant assumptions that are used for the prospective financial statements. II is wrong. Historical financial statements are not required in an attestation engagement related to prospective financial statements.

220. (B) II is correct. Consulting engagements fall under the standards of Statements on Standards for Consulting Services. I is wrong. Statements on Standards for Attestation Engagements apply to engagements involving the auditor examining internal control, pro forma financial reporting, compliance, agreed-upon procedures, forecasts, and projections.

221. (C) I and II are correct. Whenever an accountant reports on prospective financial statements, the report should include a limitation, a caveat that prospective results may not be achieved.

222. (B) II is correct. An accountant's report on a financial forecast should include a limitation on the usefulness of the report. Since a forecast contains forward-looking financial information, the limitation is in the form of a caveat that the prospective results of the financial forecast may not be achieved. I is wrong. An accountant's report on a financial forecast need not include a restriction in distribution, since a forecast can be for general use. A projection, on the other hand, needs a restriction in distribution.

223. (A) I is correct. An auditor's letter issued on significant deficiencies relating to a nonissuer's internal control observed during a financial statement audit should include a restriction on distribution. II is wrong. An auditor's letter issued on significant deficiencies relating to a nonissuer's internal control observed during a financial statement audit should indicate that the purpose of the audit was to report on the financial statements and not on internal control.

224. (C) I is correct. The auditor is required to communicate to management any significant deficiencies and material weaknesses that the auditor observes. II is correct. The auditor is required to communicate to those charged with governance (the audit committee) any significant deficiencies and material weaknesses in internal control that the auditor observes.

225. (B) II is correct. Management provides an assertion concerning the effectiveness of internal control as part of a financial statement audit of an issuer. I is wrong. Management does not automatically provide an assertion concerning the effectiveness of internal control as part of a financial statement audit of a nonissuer. Management would provide such an assertion only in a separate engagement related to internal control.

226. (A) I is correct. For a practitioner to examine and report on management's assertion about the effectiveness of an entity's internal control, the attestation engagement would have to be integrated with an audit of the entity's financial statements. This would mean that the practitioner would have to do both the audit of the financial statements and the internal control examination if the practitioner wanted to do the internal control examination. II is wrong. If the practitioner were to examine and report on management's assertion about the effectiveness of an entity's internal control, the attestation engagement report on internal control would not need to be restricted but could be made available for general distribution.

227. (A) I is correct. In the report to governance regarding significant deficiencies found in internal control during the audit of a nonissuer, the report should state that the communication is intended solely for the use of management, those charged with governance, and others within the organization. II is wrong. If Clark were to examine and report on management's assertion regarding the effectiveness of an entity's internal control, the report on internal control would not need to be restricted but could be made available for general distribution. For Clark to examine and report on management's assertion about the effectiveness of an entity's internal control, the attestation engagement would have to be integrated with an audit of the entity's financial statements. This would mean that Clark would have to do both the audit of the financial statements and the internal control examination if he wanted to report on the nonissuer's assertion regarding the client's internal control. Clark's report should include a paragraph stating that because of inherent limitations, internal control may not prevent or detect material misstatements.

228. (D) I is wrong. In the audit of a nonissuer, management is not required to assess and report on the client's internal controls. II is wrong. In the audit of a nonissuer, the auditor is not required to assess and report on the entity's internal controls. If the audit was being performed for an issuer, both management and the auditor would be required to assess and report on the entity's internal controls.

229. (B) II is correct. If the auditor detects a material misstatement and management corrects it, this would be an appropriate topic for a communication between the auditor and those charged with governance. I is wrong. The auditor may not report the absence of significant deficiencies to those charged with governance because that would imply that the auditor searched for such deficiencies.

230. (C) I is correct. Since estimates are subject to bias, the auditor should ensure that those charged with governance are informed about the basis for the auditor's conclusions regarding the reasonableness of sensitive accounting estimates. II is correct. Disagreements in the application of accounting principles relating to asset impairment or any other accounting principle should be communicated to those charged with governance.

Chapter 9: Assertions

231. (C) I is correct. Completeness is the assertion that all transactions and events have been recorded. If some have not been recorded, the books are not complete. As always with completeness, the concern is understatement. Transactions may not have been recorded when they should have been, for example, purchases and accounts payable. II is correct. Occurrence is the assertion that transactions and events that have been recorded have occurred and pertain to the company. The concern here is overstatement. If the client recorded something that has not occurred, the client has overstated. Examples include an overstatement of revenue or assets. The assertions found under the category of classes of transactions are as follows: completeness—concern is understatement; occurrence—concern is overstatement; cutoff—concern is correct period; classification—concern is correct account; and accuracy—concern is correct amount.

232. (D) I is correct. Cutoff is an assertion under classes of transactions. With the cutoff assertion, the client asserts that transactions and events have been recorded in the correct accounting period. Cutoff is closely linked with understatement and overstatement. II is correct. Completeness is another assertion under the category of classes of transactions. The assertion is that all transactions and events have been recorded. If some have not been recorded, the books are not complete. As always with completeness, the concern is understatement. Transactions may not have been recorded and they should have been, for example, purchases and accounts payable. If they were not recorded, liabilities and expenses are understated. The auditor will design tests for understatement in order to test the completeness assertion for classes of transactions. III is correct. Occurrence is the assertion that transactions and events that have been recorded have occurred and pertain to the company. The concern is overstatement. If the client recorded sales that have not yet occurred, the client has overstated. Since occurrence is an income statement assertion, the auditor's direct concern with occurrence is an overstatement of revenue on the income statement. The auditor will design tests for overstatement because an overstatement of revenue is presumed in every audit.

233. (C) I is correct. Cutoff has a direct impact on completeness and understatement. The client asserts that the proper cutoff was applied to purchases. If purchases are not recorded at year-end because the goods have not been received but title has already passed, then the books are not complete. II is correct. Cutoff also has a direct impact on occurrence and overstatement. The client asserts that the proper cutoff to sales was applied. If the client fails to use year-end as the proper cutoff, sales may be recorded prior to the earnings process. If so, sales are overstated for the period under audit, and that would impact the occurrence assertion.

234. (B) I is correct. Classification is an assertion under the category of classes of transactions and events. With classification, the client asserts that transactions have been recorded in the proper accounts—contra account and so on. For example, rather than debit sales, the company should use the contra account, sales returns, and allowances. II is correct. Accuracy is an assertion under the category of classes of transactions and events. With accuracy, the client asserts that transactions have been recorded for the proper amounts and data have been recorded accurately. III is correct. Completeness is an assertion under the category of classes of transactions. The assertion is that all transactions and events have been recorded. If some have not been recorded, the books are not complete.

235. (B) I is correct. Rights and obligations is an assertion under the category of account balances. With the rights and obligations assertion, the company asserts that it holds or controls the rights to assets and the liabilities are the obligation of the company. II is correct. Valuation is an assertion under the category of account balances. With the valuation assertion, management asserts that the assets and liabilities are properly valued and appropriately recorded. (Inventory should be recorded at the lower of cost or market, accounts receivable at the net realizable value.) III is correct. Existence is an assertion under the category of account balances. With existence, the company asserts that the asset exists. The concern is overstatement. Existence is similar if not identical to the occurrence assertion found under classes of transactions.

236. (D) I, II, III, and IV are all correct. Completeness, rights and obligations, existence, and valuation are all assertions found under the category of account balances. With completeness, the auditor's concern is understatement. The client asserts that all assets, liabilities, and equity interests that should have been recorded have been recorded. If some assets, liabilities, and equity interests have not been recorded when they should have been, the balance sheet is not complete. The auditor will perform various tests for understatement involving specific assets and liabilities to test the completeness assertion. With rights and obligations, the company asserts that it holds or controls the rights to assets and that the liabilities are the obligation of the company. The auditor's concern is that assets may be pledged as collateral and not properly disclosed. This would impact the rights and obligations assertion. The rights and obligations assertion applies to liabilities also. The client asserts that all liabilities listed are debts of the company. The auditor is concerned with the fact that a liability may be listed on the balance sheet when the liability belongs to the president of the company personally, rather than to the company itself. With existence, the client asserts that all assets, liabilities, and equity interests exist. With existence, the auditor's concern is overstatement. If assets are listed on the balance sheet when they don't exist, assets are overstated on the balance sheet and the existence assertion is affected. The auditor will test the existence assertion, testing for overstatement for specific assets. For example, when testing accounts receivable, the auditor will send confirmations to client customers to gather evidence regarding the existence of the customer. With valuation, the client asserts that assets, liabilities, and equity interests have been appropriately recorded at the proper amounts based on GAAP: inventory at the lower of cost or market, securities marked to market, and accounts receivable at the net realizable value. With valuation, the auditor's concern is that some or all of these assets may be valued incorrectly on the balance sheet; if so, the valuation assertion is affected. The auditor will test the valuation assertion with regard to specific assets and liabilities. With accounts receivable, the auditor needs to substantiate estimations regarding age of receivables and net realizable value of accounts receivable.

The auditor will also gather evidence regarding credit-granting policies of the company because if the company extends credit to just anyone, the net realizable value of accounts receivable will be overstated.

237. (A) I is correct. The existence assertion relates to the gross accounts receivable. The client asserts that all customers exist and none are fraudulent. To test the existence assertion, the auditor sends confirmations to the client's customers to ensure the existence of customer balances. II is correct. The valuation assertion relates to accounts receivable, net of the valuation allowance. The client asserts that accounts receivable is properly valued. To gather evidence to support the valuation assertion, the auditor will test the credit-granting policies of the company. The auditor wants to make sure that there is a control in place to grant credit only to approved customers and then test that control. III is correct. Rights and obligations is an assertion regarding accounts receivable. The company asserts that it has ownership rights over its accounts receivable. The auditor is concerned that some or all of the receivables have been pledged as collateral. If this has happened, the rights and obligations assertion is affected.

238. (B) II is correct. The valuation assertion relates to accounts receivable, net of the valuation allowance. To gather evidence to support the valuation assertion, the auditor will test the credit-granting policies of the company. The auditor wants to make sure that there is a control in place to grant credit only to approved customers and then test that control. I is wrong. The existence assertion relates to the gross accounts receivable, not the net. To test the existence assertion, the auditor sends confirmations to ensure the existence of customer balances.

239. (A) I is correct. If inventory was bought right before the end of Year 1 and incorrectly recorded in Year 2 (the subsequent period), the Year 1 books are not complete. In Year 1, the completeness assertion is impacted because of the understatement of inventory and related accounts payable (books are not complete). Completeness always relates to understatement. II is wrong. In the subsequent period (Year 2) there is an overstatement of inventory, which would affect the existence assertion. After Year 2, the error cancels itself out.

240. (C) I is correct. Completeness is an assertion under the category of classes of transactions and events (income statement assertions). The assertion is that all transactions and events (sales and expenses) have been recorded. If some sales and purchases have not been recorded, the books are not complete. As always with completeness, the concern is understatement. With completeness, the auditor is concerned that expenses may not have been recorded when they should have been. The auditor will perform tests to find unrecorded items. II is correct. Completeness is an assertion found under the category of account balances. Again, the auditor's concern is understatement. The client asserts that all assets, liabilities, and equity interests that should have been recorded have been recorded. If some assets, liabilities, and equity interests have not been recorded when they should have been, the balance sheet is not complete. The auditor will perform various tests for understatement involving specific assets and liabilities to test the completeness assertion.

241. (B) II is correct. Rights and obligations is an assertion found under the category of account balances (balance sheet assertions). The company asserts that it holds or controls the rights to assets and that the liabilities are the obligation of the company. The auditor's concern is that assets may be pledged as collateral and not properly disclosed. This would affect the rights and obligations assertion. The rights and obligations assertion applies to liabilities also. The client asserts that all liabilities listed are debts of the company. The auditor is concerned that a liability may be listed on the balance sheet when the liability belongs to the president of the company personally, rather than to the company itself. I is wrong. Rights and obligations is not found under the assertions about classes of transactions. Rights and obligations relate to assets and liabilities (balance sheet assertions). Assertions about classes of transactions and events relate to income statement accounts.

242. (B) II is correct. With the rights and obligations assertion, the company asserts that it holds or controls the rights to assets and that the liabilities are the obligation of the company. The rights and obligations assertion is affected in this question because the liability is listed on the balance sheet when in fact it belongs to the president of the company personally, rather than being an obligation of the company. I is wrong. While completeness is an assertion regarding account balances, completeness is a concern only when the auditor fears an understatement. In this question, the liabilities of the company are overstated, not understated, because the liability is not a corporate obligation. The rights and obligations assertion applies as does the existence assertion. The obligation should be taken off the balance sheet and not reported by the company.

243. (C) I is correct. Existence is an assertion found under the category of account balances (balance sheet assertions). The client asserts that all assets, liabilities, and equity interests exist. With existence, the auditor's concern is overstatement. If assets are listed on the balance sheet when they don't exist, or don't pertain to the company, the existence assertion is affected because the liability is overstated. In this question, the liability appears on the balance sheet but doesn't exist from the standpoint of the entity, since it belongs to the company's president. Therefore, the overstatement of the liability affects the existence assertion. Existence will always relate to overstatement. II is correct. With the rights and obligations assertion, the company asserts that it holds or controls the rights to assets and that the liabilities are the obligation of the company. The rights and obligations are affected in this question because the liability is listed on the balance sheet when in fact it belongs to the president of the company personally, rather than being an obligation of the company.

244. (D) I is wrong. It is not a rights and obligations issue unless the debt is not a company debt and it is included either fraudulently or erroneously on the balance sheet. In this question, the debt is a company debt. II is wrong. Completeness is concerned with understatement of debt, not overstatement. Since the company debt is overstated on the balance sheet, the existence assertion is affected.

245. (A) I is correct. Completeness is an assertion found under the category of account balances. Johnson Corp. asserts that all assets, liabilities, and equity interests that should have been recorded have been recorded. If some assets, liabilities, and equity interests have not been recorded when they should have been, the balance sheet is not complete. In this question, the accounting department of Johnson Corp. thought the debt was that of the president, so the debt was left off the balance sheet of Johnson Corp. As a result, the books are not complete. II is wrong. Existence is an assertion found under the category of account balances (balance sheet assertions). The client asserts that all assets, liabilities, and equity interests exist. With existence, the auditor's concern is overstatement. In this question, the auditor is concerned with understatement, not overstatement.

246. (B) II is correct. Valuation is an assertion found under the category of account balances (balance sheet assertions). With this assertion, the client asserts that assets, liabilities, and equity interests have been appropriately recorded at the proper amounts based on GAAP. Therefore, if the auditor has decided that inventory is based on a variation of FIFO and LIFO that is not viewed as GAAP, then the inventory is not properly valued. I is wrong. Rights and obligations is also found under the category of account balances (balance sheet assertions). With the rights and obligations assertion, the company asserts that it holds or controls the rights to the assets and that the liabilities listed on the balance sheet are the obligation of the company. In this question, there is no evidence to suggest that the inventory is not that of the company.

247. (B) II is correct. Valuation is an assertion found under the category of account balances (balance sheet assertions). The client asserts that assets, liabilities, and equity interests have been appropriately recorded at the proper amounts based on GAAP. If the auditor has decided that inventory is based on a FIFO and LIFO method that is not viewed as proper accounting, the inventory is not properly valued. I is wrong. While completeness is an assertion found under the category of account balances, completeness would affect inventory only if the inventory were understated based on incorrect cutoff. In this question the inventory is overstated based on incorrect cutoff. Therefore, the existence assertion would be affected rather than the completeness assertion.

248. (C) I is correct. With completeness, the client asserts that all inventory and the related accounts payable have been recorded. If some inventory has not been recorded due to incorrect cutoff, the books are not complete. Since the incorrect cutoff led to the understatement, the completeness assertion is affected. II is correct. Valuation is an assertion found under the category of account balances (balance sheet assertions). The client asserts that assets, liabilities, and equity interests have been appropriately recorded at the proper amounts based on GAAP. If the auditor has decided that inventory is based on a FIFO and LIFO method that is not viewed as proper accounting, the inventory is not properly valued; therefore, the valuation assertion is affected.

249. (B) II is correct. Occurrence is an assertion found in the category known as classes of transactions and events (income statement assertions). With the occurrence assertion, the client asserts that transactions and events that have been recorded on the income statement have actually occurred. If the client recorded sales on the income statement but the sales have not yet occurred, the client has overstated sales and affected the occurrence assertion for sales. The concern with occurrence is an overstatement of revenue. The auditor will design tests for overstatement because an overstatement of revenue is presumed in every audit. I is wrong. Existence is a balance sheet assertion, not an income statement assertion. While recording sales prior to the earnings process being complete would affect the existence assertion due to an overstatement of accounts receivable at year-end, the question asks which income statement assertion is affected and existence is not an income statement assertion.

250. (C) I is correct. Occurrence is an assertion found in the category known as classes of transactions and events (income statement assertions). With the occurrence assertion, the client asserts that transactions and events that have been recorded on the income statement have actually occurred. The concern is overstatement. If the client recorded sales on the income statement but they have not yet occurred, the client has overstated sales and the occurrence assertion for sales is affected. The auditor will test the occurrence assertion for sales because an overstatement of revenue is presumed in every audit. II is correct. Existence is an assertion found under the category of account balances (balance sheet assertions). The client asserts that all assets, liabilities, and equity interests exist. With existence, the auditor's concern is overstatement of assets. If assets are listed on the balance sheet but they don't exist, the existence assertion is affected. If the account receivable is recorded prior to the earnings process being complete, assets are overstated. Existence is similar to occurrence, as they both relate to overstatement, but existence relates to overstatement of assets (existence is a balance sheet assertion) whereas occurrence relates to overstatement of revenue (occurrence is an income statement assertion).

251. (A) I is correct. Rights and obligations is an assertion found under the category of account balances (balance sheet assertions). With the rights and obligations assertion, the company asserts that it holds or controls the rights to the assets and that the liabilities listed on the balance sheet are the obligation of the company. In this question, the building recorded on the balance sheet of Andrinua Corp. belongs to Desimone Inc., so Andrinua Corp. has no rights of ownership and should not include the building on its balance sheet. Thus, the rights and obligations assertion is affected. II is wrong. Completeness is an assertion found under the category of account balances. Andrinua asserts that all assets that should have been recorded have been recorded. If some assets have not been recorded when they should have been recorded, the balance sheet is not complete. With completeness, the auditor's concern is understatement. In this question, however, the asset was recorded but should not have been. Therefore, overstatement is a concern, not understatement.

252. (C) I is correct. Completeness is an assertion found under the category of presentation and disclosure. The client asserts that all disclosures are complete. If any material items that should have been disclosed were not disclosed, the footnotes are not complete. Once again with completeness, the concern is understatement. II is correct. Classification and understandability is an assertion under the category of presentation and disclosure. Liabilities that mature in less than one year should be classified as current liabilities rather than long term. Assets that are liquid should be classified as current assets. Assets that are not intended to be liquidated within a year should be reported as long term. Understandability relates to information being presented and described clearly. For example, related-party footnotes—including the nature of the relationship, who the parties are (buyer and seller), and the dollar amount of each related-party transaction—must be understood by nonaccountants. The assertions found under the category of presentation and disclosure are occurrence, rights and obligations, completeness, classification and understandability, and accuracy and valuation.

253. (A) I is correct. Completeness is found in all three categories of assertions. With classes of transactions and events (income statement assertions), the client asserts that all revenue and expenses have been recorded. If some have not, the income statement is not complete. With assertions regarding account balances (balance sheet assertions), the client asserts that all assets, liabilities, and equity accounts have been recorded. If some assets, liabilities, and equity accounts have not been recorded, the books are not complete. With the assertion category known as presentation and disclosure, the client asserts that the footnotes are complete. II is wrong. Rights and obligations is an assertion found under the category of account balances (balance sheet assertions) and also presentation and disclosure. It is not found under the assertion category known as classes of transactions and events (income statement assertions).

254. (B) II is correct. Classification is an assertion under the category of classes of transactions and events (income statement assertions). With classification, the client asserts that the transactions were recorded using the correct accounts. If equipment was purchased and it was recorded as inventory, the classification assertion is affected. I is wrong. With rights and obligations, the concern is that the asset that was recorded is not owned by the company. In this question, the asset is owned by the company; it is just not classified properly.

255. (C) III is correct. Completeness, while an assertion, is not an assertion category. Completeness is found in all three assertion categories: classes of transaction and events, account balances, and presentation and disclosure. I is wrong. Presentation and disclosure is an assertion category relating to footnotes and presentation of items in the financial statements. II is wrong. Classes of transactions and events is an assertion category, relating mostly to income statement accounts.

Chapter 10: Evidence Gathering and Transaction Cycles, Part 1

256. (B) II is correct. In the phrase "nature, extent, and timing" of audit procedures, the term *nature* refers to the type of test performed, whether the test is a test of controls or perhaps a substantive test. I is wrong. In the phrase "nature, extent, and timing" of audit procedures, the term *nature* does not refer to the amount of testing. The term *extent* refers to the amount of testing.

257. (B) II is correct. Lapping involves the theft of receivables by an employee. The employee then must cover the theft by giving credit to the customer who paid. However, lapping results in a delay in the recording of specific credits to customer accounts because today's collection covers up yesterday's theft. Lapping can be prevented by proper segregation of duties. The same employee should not be able to both deposit customer checks and post the credits to the customer accounts. I is wrong. Kiting has nothing to do with receivables. Kiting involves cash that appears to be in two company bank accounts at the same time.

258. (B) III is correct. The same employee should not be able to both deposit customer checks and post the credits to the customer accounts. If the same employee were able to do both, the employee could both steal from the company and cover up the theft in the accounting records. If one employee were in position to do both jobs, mandatory vacation would help to prevent and detect such potential theft of receivables, known as lapping. I is wrong. The employee who opens the mail should deposit the customer checks into Arthur's bank accounts, but first the employee should prepare a listing of all checks received that day. II is wrong. The employee who opens the mail should prepare a listing of all checks received that day, known as a duplicate check listing.

259. (C) In a revenue cycle, for proper segregation of duties, the sales department will prepare the initial sales order, quantity, price, color, and so on, but a separate department will authorize the customer's credit. Since most companies ship the goods to the customer prior to receiving payment, the independent auditor tests to see if there is a policy in place within the organization to verify customer credit before shipping goods. Therefore, answers A, B, and D are wrong.

260. (D) I is wrong. Orders of merchandise should not lead directly to goods being shipped; some verification needs to be made of the credit worthiness of the customer. The credit department, not the billings department, will maintain a credit file for this purpose. The file will contain a credit report for the customer, the history of payments, and possibly financial statements if the customer buys large amounts. II is wrong. The billings department does not prepare the bill of lading; rather, the shipping department prepares the bill of lading. The billings department prepares the sales invoice.

261. (C) I is correct. The shipping department needs a copy of the approved sales order to serve as authorization for shipment of the goods to the customer. II is correct. The billings department needs a copy of the approved sales order to serve as authorization to prepare the sales invoice and send it to the customer so that the company can get paid. Payment won't happen until a copy of the bill of lading is received by the billings department to serve as evidence of the shipment.

262. (B) II is correct. In the revenue cycle, the billings department prepares the sales invoice and sends a copy to the customer so the company can get paid. The sales invoice is prepared by the billings department but not before the billings department receives a copy of the sales order. III is correct. In the revenue cycle, the billings department prepares the sales invoice and sends a copy to the customer so the company can get paid. The sales invoice is prepared by the billings department but not before the billings department receives a copy of the bill of lading indicating that goods were shipped. I is wrong. The purchase requisition is not part of the revenue cycle; instead, purchase requisition is part of the purchasing cycle.

263. (B) The billings department keeps a pending, or open, file. No action is taken by the billings department until a copy of both the sales order and the bill of lading are received. Then, the billings department compares the sales order to the bill of lading in a process called reconciliation. The billings department is an example of the accounting function. If the billings department determines that the shipment was authorized and the two documents reconcile, the billings department will prepare a sales invoice and send a copy to the customer so the entity can get paid. A is wrong. The sales department prepares the sales order but does not need a copy of the bill of lading. C is wrong. The credit department approves customer credit before shipment if the order is over a certain dollar amount, but the credit department would not need a copy of the bill of lading. D is wrong. The warehouse does not need a copy of the bill of lading. The warehouse department maintains custody of the goods and can only transfer the goods within the organization, usually to the shipping department. The shipping department, rather than the warehouse, prepares the bill of lading and ships the goods.

264. (D) A copy of the sales order and bill of lading is sent to the billings department. The billings department is an accounting function. In this department, they match the information on the sales order with the bill of lading and verify that each is properly authorized. This process is called reconciliation. If everything is in agreement, the billings department prepares the sales invoice and records the sales invoice into the sales journal. Therefore, A, B, and C are wrong.

265. (D) Within a proper segregation of duties for the revenue cycle, the warehouse department is charged with custody of the merchandise until an approved sales order is received from the credit department. Then the warehouse department sends the ordered goods within the organization to the shipping department to ready the goods for transport. A is wrong. The shipping department is not charged with custody of the goods but rather with reconciliation and execution. Before shipping but after receiving the goods from the warehouse, the shipping department matches the sales order received from the warehouse with the sales order received from the credit department. This process is known as reconciliation. Only if the two sales orders agree on quantity and type of goods are the goods readied and shipped. B is wrong. The billings department is an example of accounting, not custody. Within the revenue cycle, the billings department prepares the sales invoice and records the sale. C is wrong. The receiving room is not part of the revenue cycle. The receiving room is part of the purchasing cycle.

266. (D) I is correct. The warehouse department is charged with custody of the merchandise until an approved sales order is received from the credit department. Then the warehouse department normally transfers the goods within the organization to the shipping department to ready the goods for transport. III is correct. Within a purchasing cycle, the receiving room takes initial receipt of merchandise that arrives from the vendor. After making an independent count of the goods received, the receiving room normally transfers these newly received goods within the organization to the warehouse department. II is wrong. The shipping department will normally transport goods outside the organization.

267. (A) Within a proper segregation of duties for the revenue cycle, the credit department is charged with authorization. In most companies, goods are shipped to the customer before the selling company gets paid. Therefore, only if the credit department approves the customer for credit should goods be transferred from the warehouse and shipped to the customer. If the credit department denies the customer's credit, the goods should not be transferred from the warehouse to the shipping department, or shipped to the customer. B is wrong. The billings department is an accounting function. The billings department will prepare the sales invoice after receiving a copy of the approved sales order from credit and a copy of the bill of lading from shipping. If the two documents match, the sales invoice should be prepared by the billings department and sent to the customer so that the company can get paid. C is wrong. The purchasing department is not part of the revenue cycle. D is wrong. The shipping department is an example of reconciliation and execution, not authorization. Before shipping, the shipping department reconciles a copy of the approved sales order received from the credit department with the sales order received from the warehouse. If the two sales orders match, with the same amount and type of goods, then the goods are gathered and shipped to the customer.

268. (D) Within the revenue cycle, for proper segregation of duties, the bill of lading, a shipping document, is prepared by the shipping department and the sales invoice is prepared by the billings or accounting department. Therefore, A, B, and C are wrong.

269. (C) I is correct. Whenever any asset is conveyed within a company, the recipient should inspect the goods for damage. This procedure is an important internal control to detect mistakes and problems before the asset moves any further within the system. II is correct. Whenever any asset is conveyed within a company, the recipient should count and verify the description with the related documentation. This procedure is an important internal control to detect mistakes and problems before the asset moves any further within the system.

270. (C) I is correct. A perpetual inventory system maintains a constant record of the inventory on hand. As goods are shipped, the inventory records should be reduced accordingly. Therefore, a copy of each bill of lading should be forwarded to the inventory department for this purpose. II is correct. The billings department needs a copy of the bill of lading in order to prepare the sales invoice. It is not enough for the billings department to have a copy of the approved sales order. A copy of the bill of lading is also needed to serve as evidence that the goods were shipped and that the sales order was not only approved but fully executed.

271. (A) In a revenue cycle, the sales order is prepared first, followed by the bill of lading, and then the sales invoice. Therefore, B, C, and D are wrong.

272. (B) The warehouse department does not prepare the sales order, the sales invoice, or the bill of lading. The warehouse prepares a warehouse receipt that serves as evidence that the warehouse transferred the goods ordered to the shipping department. The warehouse transfers goods only within the organization. The shipping department conveys merchandise to appropriate outside parties. Internal control is strengthened by having these departments independent of each other; thus, goods cannot be removed from the company without having two departments involved. This arrangement offers a system of checks and balances. A is wrong. The sales department prepares the sales order. C is wrong. The shipping department prepares the bill of lading. D is wrong. The billings department prepares the sales invoice.

273. (C) I is correct. If the auditor begins with entries in the sales journal and makes sure that there is a sales invoice to support it, this would be a test of the occurrence or existence assertion. The auditor is testing for overstatement of sales. An auditor always begins with the event that has presumed to have taken place—in this case, that revenue was recorded—and moves to the event that is uncertain—that a sale actually occurred. II is correct. If an auditor begins with entries in the sales journal and makes sure that there is a sales invoice to support it, the auditor is searching for overstatement of revenue. If the auditor finds an entry in the sales journal with no supporting sales invoice, sales are overstated.

274. (A) I is correct. If an auditor begins with a sample of bills of lading and traces forward into the accounting records, the auditor is testing completeness of sales, or understatement. The auditor always begins with the event that is assumed to have taken place—in this case, that goods were shipped—and moves to the event that is uncertain—that sales invoices were prepared. II is wrong. If there is no sales invoice found for a particular bill of lading, the auditor fears that sales may be understated, not overstated. For each bill of lading, the auditor expects to find a sales invoice and an entry in the sales journal that records that invoice. For any bill of lading where a sales invoice isn't found, the auditor suspects that the shipment was either a fraudulent shipment involving theft of goods or, possibly, a consignment shipment, in which case the client shipped goods to a potential customer but cannot record the sale until the potential customer resells the goods.

275. (C) I is correct. For each bill of lading, the auditor expects to find a sales invoice and an entry in the sales journal that records that invoice. For any bill of lading where a sales invoice isn't found, the auditor suspects that the shipment may be a fraudulent shipment involving theft of goods. II is correct. For each bill of lading, the auditor expects to find a sales invoice and an entry in the sales journal that records that sales invoice. For any bill of lading where a sales invoice isn't found, the auditor suspects that the shipment was fraudulent or, possibly, a consignment shipment, in which case the client shipped goods to a potential customer but cannot record the sale until the potential customer resells the goods. Since a consignment shipment involves a transfer of possession but not title, no sales invoice would be found. The auditor would request a list of consignment shipments.

276. **(C)** I is correct. The auditor wants to know, if a sales invoice is prepared, were the goods actually ordered and shipped? The auditor should start by selecting a sample from the sales invoices and look to see if there are shipping documents to support the sales invoices. The auditor always starts with the event that is assumed to have happened and moves to the event that is uncertain. II is correct. If the auditor finds sales invoices with no related shipping documents, this would be a test for overstatement of sales, rather than understatement. The occurrence assertion is affected rather than the completeness assertion when the fear is overstatement.

277. **(A)** I is correct. The auditor wants to know, if goods are ordered and shipped, was an invoice sent and a record made? The auditor should select a sample of bills of lading and verify that corresponding sales invoices are properly prepared and recorded. II is wrong. Consignment shipments could explain why goods were shipped but not recorded as a sale, since consignment shipments involve a transfer of possession but not title.

278. **(A)** I is correct. Starting with the source documents and tracing forward to the sales invoice means that the auditor is concerned with understatement—in this case, understatement of revenue. A shipment of merchandise where no sales invoice is found could be an indication of a fraudulent shipment. The concern with understatement of revenue is the possible theft of merchandise. II is wrong. Starting with the shipping documents and looking for sales invoices means that the auditor is concerned with understatement of revenue, not overstatement of revenue. While the auditor will certainly perform audit procedures to gather evidence regarding overstatement of revenue, this test is for understatement of revenue. An auditor begins with the event that has presumed to have taken place—that goods were shipped—and moves to the event that is uncertain—that sales were recorded.

279. **(D)** I is wrong. Any test looking for support for a recorded balance in a journal or ledger provides evidence about the existence or occurrence assertion, not completeness. When performing two-directional testing, an auditor begins with the event that is assumed to have taken place—that sales were recorded—and moves to the event that is uncertain—that goods were shipped. II is wrong. If an auditor starts with the entries in the sales journal and seeks supporting documentation to corroborate, the auditor would be more interested in finding shipping documents that correspond to the recorded sale, not just sales orders. Shipping documents are greater evidence that the sale was fully executed, while sales orders prove only that the customer intended to buy. Only if the credit department approves the customer should the sale be fully executed and shipped. Therefore, the auditor would want to find both the bill of lading and the sales order for even greater evidence that the sale occurred.

280. **(C)** To detect a possible understatement of sales, an auditor would trace from the shipping documents to the sales invoice to see if the items shipped (and presumably sold) have been recorded. The auditor always begins a two-directional test by starting with the event that is presumed to have taken place—that goods were shipped—and moves to the event that is uncertain—that sales were recorded. In this case the auditor is testing forward. Any two-directional test that moves forward is a test for completeness, or understatement. A is wrong. Starting with the sales invoice and moving to the shipping documents is a backward-directional test. Testing backward is a test for occurrence or existence, that is, overstatement. B and D are wrong because moving from one journal to another is not a test for understatement or overstatement.

281. (C) I is correct. In the subsequent period, the auditor looks at certain types of transactions because they can help to substantiate the balances reported on the financial statements. With accounts receivable, examining how much bad debt was written off shortly after year-end is a substantive test for accounts receivable in the subsequent period because it provides evidence as to valuation assertion for accounts receivable. Accounts receivable must have been overvalued at year-end by the amount written off early in January. II is correct. In the subsequent period, the auditor looks at certain types of transactions because they can help to substantiate the balances reported on the financial statements. If a customer pays in January, the customer must have owed in December, which means the customer must have existed in December. Therefore, examining cash collections a few days after year-end provides evidence regarding the existence assertion for accounts receivable.

282. (B) II is correct. In the subsequent period, the auditor looks at certain types of transactions because they can help to substantiate the balances reported on the financial statements. If a customer pays in January, the customer must have owed in December, which means the customer must have existed in December. Therefore, examining cash collections a few days after year-end provides evidence regarding the existence assertion for accounts receivable. I is wrong. In the subsequent period, the auditor looks at certain types of transactions because they can help to substantiate the balances reported on the financial statements. With accounts receivable, examining how much bad debt was written off shortly after year-end provides evidence as to valuation assertion. However, it provides no evidence regarding existence of the customer, which is what the question asks about. To test the existence assertion for accounts receivable in the subsequent period, examine cash collections in January.

283. (D) The completeness assertion is tested whenever the auditor tests forward. A test that starts with the sales invoice and moves to the sales journal is a test going forward because the sales invoice is created and then the sales invoice is recorded in the sales journal. In a two-directional test, an auditor starts with the event that is presumed to have taken place—in this case, that sales invoices were created—and then moves to the event that is uncertain—that sales invoices were recorded. A is wrong. The occurrence assertion would be tested if the auditor began with entries in the sales journal and looked for evidence that the sales occurred, the goods were shipped, and the sales were invoiced. This would be a test for overstatement. B is wrong. The classification assertion would be tested by the auditor looking to see if the client used a contra-account for sales returns and not just decreased the sales account for every sales return. C is wrong. Accuracy would be tested if the auditor recomputed amounts on the sales invoices.

284. (B) II is correct. Tracing sales orders to the revenue account provides evidence concerning the completeness assertion of the revenue account. The auditor begins with the event that is presumed to have taken place—that goods were ordered—and moves to the event that is uncertain—that sales were recorded. I is wrong. Tracing sales orders to the revenue account provides no evidence that approved spending limits are exceeded. If approved spending limits are exceeded, this would be the result of management override of internal control, but this would not be detected by the auditor tracing sales orders to the revenue account.

285. (B) II is correct. External confirmations provide evidence to support the existence assertion. Confirmations are meant to ascertain that the balances shown on the company's records actually do exist; the customer is real and not fictitious. For this reason, the auditor mails confirmations to the client's customers and the customers are asked to respond directly to the auditor so that the client cannot intervene. I is wrong. External confirmations provide little evidence as to whether accounts will actually be collected and, therefore, are not particularly helpful in estimating net realizable value. Valuation assertion for accounts receivable is tested by checking the client's credit-granting policies and by reading contractual agreements regarding pledging of receivables as well as by examining bad write-offs in the subsequent period.

286. (A) I is correct. External confirmations provide evidence to support the existence assertion. External confirmations are meant to ascertain that the balances shown on the company's records actually do exist; the customer is real and not fictitious. For this reason, the auditor mails the confirmations to the client's customers and the customers are asked to respond directly to the auditor so that the client cannot intervene. The auditor should be in charge of mailing the confirmations to ensure that they actually do get mailed. Either the auditor or the client can prepare the confirmations, but if the client is involved, the auditor should make a careful review. Because of confidentiality, a representative of the client must sign the confirmations, but all other actions are taken by the auditor, both the mailing and the receiving of the responses. II is wrong. Credit verification refers to the valuation of accounts receivable. By checking credit before shipping goods, the client is trying to minimize the likelihood of selling goods and then having to write off the debt as uncollectible. Any question about accounts receivable that deals with the uncollectible accounts or the aging schedule deals with the valuation assertion rather than existence.

287. (C) I is correct. Positive confirmations ask for a response in every case so that more tangible evidence is obtained. II is correct. Positive confirmations are more likely to be used when inherent and control risks have been assessed as high and the acceptable level of detection risk has been lowered. Negative confirmations are used when risks are low. Note that both positive and negative confirmations can be used in the same audit.

288. (D) I is wrong. For good internal controls, the credit manager should be independent of the sales function. If the credit manager reported to the vice president of sales, the vice president of sales would be able to influence the credit manager to relax the standards and approve more customers for credit in order to increase sales. II is wrong. The credit manager should not authorize a bad debt write-off. The authorization for a bad debt write-off should come from a higher source, someone independent of the sales function. The treasurer normally authorizes a bad debt write-off, not the credit manager.

289. (C) Both I and II are correct. As indicated by the following table, if ending inventory is overstated, cost of goods sold is understated; therefore, gross profit, and ultimately net income, is too high.

Beginning inventory	0
Purchases	10
Less ending inventory	**4**
Cost of goods sold	**6**
Sales	25
Less cost of goods sold	**6**
Gross profit	**19**

290. (C) I is correct. Goods shipped out on consignment still belong to the consignor; that is, no title passes, only possession. II is correct. When an auditor examines a client's inventory, items shipped out on consignment by the client still belong to the client, so the rights and obligations assertion is affected. The client still has rights of ownership even after the consignment shipment.

291. (B) II is correct. The receiving department gets a copy of the purchase order with the quantity ordered deliberately missing. The receiving department needs a copy of the purchase order to know what kind of goods to expect delivery of, but if the receiving room doesn't know how many units are being delivered, the workers there are forced to perform a more accurate independent count. I is wrong. The receiving department does not need a copy of the purchase requisition. The purchase requisition is needed only so that someone within the organization cannot both authorize and execute a purchase of goods from outside the entity.

292. (B) Four documents are involved in a typical purchasing cycle: purchase requisition, purchase order, receiving report, and purchase invoice. The purchase requisition could be prepared by anyone but then needs to be approved by that person's department head. The purchase order is prepared in the purchasing department. The receiving report is prepared by the receiving room. The purchase invoice is prepared outside the organization.

293. (A) In a purchasing cycle, the first document prepared is the purchase requisition (IV). The requisition is prepared by someone in the company that is requesting an item and is first sent to that individual's supervisor for approval. The approved requisition is then sent to the warehouse to see if the item is in stock and can be transferred within the company from the warehouse to the department that requested the item. If the item is not in stock, the purchasing department gets involved and orders the item from outside the company. This department prepares the purchase order (I). When the purchased item arrives, a receiving report (II) is then prepared by the receiving room. Eventually, a purchase invoice (III) will arrive from the vendor.

294. (D) A pending (or open) file is maintained in accounts or vouchers payable to gather the four documents: purchase requisition, purchase order, receiving report, and purchase invoice. When all are eventually received, they are matched by accounts payable and the authorizations are checked. Then, a voucher is prepared by accounts payable. The voucher is the approval for payment. A is wrong. The purchasing department prepares the purchase order but does not authorize payment. B is wrong. The billings department is not part of the purchasing cycle. The billings department is found in the revenue cycle and prepares the sales invoice. C is wrong. The receiving room prepares the receiving report but has no authorization to approve payment for goods.

295. (D) I is wrong. If goods are accepted by the receiving room, receiving room personnel complete a receiving report to provide all information on the merchandise, the quantity received, and so on. A copy of the receiving report goes to accounts payable, which now gets its third document and keeps the file open with the three documents in it until the fourth document, the purchase invoice, is received. II is wrong. The department that originally requested the merchandise will also get a copy of the receiving report. Whatever department within the company originally requested the item needs to know that it came in so that the department can put it out for sale.

296. (C) II is correct. The purchase invoice is prepared outside the organization by the vendor. III is correct. The purchase requisition is prepared by the department within the organization that requests an item be purchased. This is normally an item that needs to be purchased for resale. I is wrong. The purchase order is the only document prepared by the purchasing department.

297. (B) I is correct. The purchase invoice is prepared outside the organization. This is important because documents generated outside the organization are generally considered to be more persuasive audit evidence than documents generated within the organization. II is wrong. The receiving report is prepared within the organization, in the receiving room, when the purchased items arrive. After the receiving department counts the items in, department personnel prepare the receiving report without knowing how many goods were ordered. III is wrong. The voucher package is prepared by the vouchers payable or accounts payable department. The voucher package contains copies of the purchase requisition, the purchase order, the receiving report, and the purchase invoice. Once accounts payable has all four documents, they can reconcile the documents and prepare the voucher package.

298. (A) I is correct. The vouchers payable department approves vendors' invoices for payment. Before approval, the purchase invoice should be compared with the purchase order and receiving report, the supporting documents. If all documents match and are properly authorized, the vouchers or accounts payable department prepares the voucher, which is the approval for payment to the vendor. II is wrong. Deliberately removing the quantity ordered on the receiving department copy of the purchase order is a desirable internal control procedure, but it is typically performed by the purchasing department, not vouchers payable.

299. (C) While vouchers payable typically prepares the approval for payment, called the voucher, the voucher is then sent to the cash disbursements department for payment. The check to the vendor is ultimately cut in the cash disbursements department, not vouchers or accounts payable. This is an example of a segregation of duties between authorization and execution. Vouchers payable authorizes the payment; cash disbursements makes the payment. Therefore, A, B, and D are wrong.

300. (A) I is correct. A copy of the purchase order is attached to the voucher and becomes part of the backup documentation. The voucher is the document that acknowledges the liability and approves payment. The backup documentation consists of copies of the purchase requisition, purchase order, receiving report, and purchase invoice. The four forms are attached in what is sometimes called a voucher package. The voucher package is sent to the cash disbursements department for payment. II is correct. A copy of the receiving report is attached to the voucher and becomes part of the backup documentation. III is wrong. The bill of lading is not a document in the purchasing cycle, but rather a document in the sales cycle.

301. (D) I is correct. The voucher is the document that acknowledges the liability and approves payment. A company uses a voucher system as a control to prevent money from leaving the company without proper authorization. The voucher has to be prepared, signed, and forwarded to cash disbursements in order for payment to be made to the vendor. II is correct. The backup documentation (all four forms) is attached to the voucher in what is sometimes called a voucher package. III is correct. The voucher is recorded in the voucher register, which is summarized periodically for recording in the general ledger by general accounting. The voucher package is forwarded to the cash disbursements department for payment.

302. (C) The cash disbursements department both signs the check and mails the check to the vendor. Good internal controls dictate that once a check is signed, it should be mailed immediately and not travel backward through the system. Vouchers payable prepares the voucher and forwards the voucher to the cash disbursements department. Usually the check is signed by the treasurer in the cash disbursements department. The check should be mailed out immediately once signed. Therefore, A, B, and D are wrong.

303. (A) In the cash disbursements department, the check is signed and the voucher is perforated or marked as "paid" so that the voucher won't be paid twice. The check is recorded in the check register (or cash disbursements journal) and the check is quickly mailed after it has been signed. B is wrong. Vouchers payable prepares the voucher and records the voucher in the voucher register, but vouchers payable does not cancel or perforate the voucher. The department that pays the bill should cancel the voucher, and that department is cash disbursements. C is wrong. The purchasing department prepares the purchase order but does not prepare the voucher or perforate the voucher. D is wrong. The receiving department does not even get a copy of the voucher. Receiving gets a copy of the purchase order with the number of units ordered deliberately left blank to force an accurate count of the goods by receiving. Receiving is then forced to count the goods in and prepare a receiving report based on what was counted in.

304. (C) I is correct. In an audit, in the evidence-gathering stage of the purchasing cycle, the auditor would examine a sample of paid vouchers to gather evidence as to whether each voucher is supported by a vendor invoice. Any paid voucher that is not supported by a vendor invoice could be a fraudulent payment and someone may be stealing from the company. II is correct. In an audit, in the evidence-gathering stage of the purchasing cycle, the auditor would examine a sample of paid vouchers to gather evidence as to whether each voucher is perforated or marked as paid so that the voucher will be paid only once.

305. (B) II is correct. To provide assurance that each voucher is submitted and paid only once, an auditor would examine a sample of paid vouchers and determine whether each voucher is perforated or marked as paid. Once marked as paid, the voucher will not be paid again. I is wrong. While the auditor would examine a sample of paid vouchers to gather evidence as to whether each voucher is supported by a vendor invoice, making sure that each voucher is supported by a vendor's invoice would show authorization but not any evidence of double payment.

306. (A) I is correct. When an auditor vouches a sample of entries in the voucher register to the supporting documents, this procedure is testing whether recorded entries are valid, that is, whether they did exist. The auditor always starts with the event that is presumed to have taken place—in this case, that a voucher was recorded—and moves to the event that is uncertain—that goods were ordered and received. II is wrong. When an auditor vouches a sample of entries in the voucher register to the supporting documents, this procedure is testing whether recorded entries are valid, NOT whether valid entries were recorded. With completeness, the concern is understatement, but this question asks about overstatement.

307. (D) II is correct. The accounts payable, or vouchers payable, department has the responsibility to prepare vouchers for payment. As part of that process, an employee in the vouchers payable (or accounts payable) department should check vendors' invoices for math accuracy by recomputing calculations and extensions, and should match the vendors' invoices with receiving reports and purchase orders for quantities, prices, and terms. Only after this reconciliation process should the voucher be prepared. I is wrong, the purchasing department selects the vendor and prepares the purchase order and ultimately executes the purchase. III is wrong, Cash disbursements takes the approved voucher from the vouchers payable department, signs the check, and then immediately mails the check to the vendor and cancels the voucher so that the voucher cannot be paid twice.

308. (A) I is correct. In the purchasing cycle, the receiving report is prepared by the receiving room. II is wrong. The bill of lading is a document in the revenue cycle, not the purchasing cycle. In the revenue cycle, the bill of lading serves as evidence of a shipment of goods.

309. (C) I is correct. In testing completeness for accounts payable, the auditor will choose a selection of purchase invoices and make sure that any obligation is recorded properly. The auditor starts with the supporting documentation and looks to see if the transaction was properly recorded. Any test that moves forward is testing completeness, or understatement. The auditor starts with the event that is assumed to have happened—in this case, that goods were purchased and a debt was incurred—and moves to the event that is uncertain—that the debt was recorded. II is correct. In testing completeness for accounts payable, the auditor will choose a selection of receiving reports and make sure that any goods received were recorded and any obligation is recorded properly. When the auditor starts with the supporting documentation and looks to see if the transaction was properly recorded, this is a test for understatement, or completeness.

310. (A) I is correct. When an auditor traces a sample of purchase orders and the related receiving reports to the purchases journal and the cash disbursements journal, the auditor is testing to see if transactions were recorded. The client asserts that all transactions that should have been recorded have been recorded. If some have not been recorded, the books are not complete. The auditor starts with the event that is assumed to have happened—that goods were purchased and received and a debt was incurred—and moves to the event that is uncertain—that the debt was recorded. II is wrong. When the auditor starts with the supporting documentation and looks to see if the transaction was properly recorded, this is a test for completeness (understatement), not existence.

311. (B) II is correct. Testing the existence or occurrence assertion, the auditor starts with the general ledger balance and vouches backward, seeking support. The client asserts that all recorded transactions were valid. If any transactions that were recorded did not actually exist, the books are overstated. The auditor starts with the event that is assumed to have happened—in this case, that purchases were recorded—and moves to the event that is uncertain—that goods were ordered and received. I is wrong. In the purchasing cycle, when the auditor is testing the existence or occurrence assertion, he or she does not start with the supporting documents. Starting with the supporting documents is a test for completeness.

312. (B) II is correct. Receiving reports are client-generated documents in the purchasing cycle. I is wrong. Bills of lading, although they may be generated by the client, are documents generated in the sales cycle, not the purchasing cycle.

313. (D) I is wrong. Vendor invoices and packing slips are generated by vendors. II is wrong. Bills of lading may be generated by the client, but accounts receivable confirmations are not generated by the client. They are auditor generated. To be considered valid evidence, accounts receivable confirmations should be between the auditor and the client's customer.

314. (B) The purchase invoice should indicate the FOB point when title changed hands, and the receiving report should indicate the date of receipt of the goods. These documents would enable the auditor to determine the date on which the liability was incurred to ensure that it occurred in the period it was recorded in and that the inventory exists in the current period. A, C, and D are wrong.

315. (B) II is correct. Unrecorded liabilities eventually become due and must be paid. A review of cash disbursements after the balance sheet date is an effective procedure for detecting unrecorded liabilities. I is wrong. Starting with a sample of accounts payable entries recorded just before year-end will not provide evidence regarding what should have been recorded. Starting with a sample of accounts payable entries recorded just before year-end would be helpful to gather evidence regarding what should not have been recorded.

316. (C) Both I and II are correct. Observation of physical inventory counts provides evidence about both existence and completeness. Observing the inventory provides evidence that it physically exists; observing the actual count provides evidence regarding completeness (i.e., does it appear that the client is doing a careful, accurate, and complete job of counting all of the inventory?).

317. (D) I is wrong. An auditor cannot determine whether there have been changes in pricing methods simply by observing a client's physical inventories. II is wrong. An auditor cannot determine whether outstanding purchase commitments exist simply by observing a client's physical inventories.

318. (C) Both I and II are correct. Rights and obligations might be tested by examining paid vendors' invoices, by inspecting consignment agreements and contracts, or by confirming inventory held at outside locations.

319. (D) An auditor's observation procedures with respect to well-kept perpetual inventories that are periodically checked by physical counts may be performed before, during, or after the end of the audit period. If, however, the assessed level of control risk for inventory is high, the observation procedures should be performed at year-end.

320. (D) The auditor should observe the inventory count of goods held in a public warehouse if the inventory held there is significant; otherwise, confirmation of such inventory is sufficient. The auditor's personal observation is generally one of the most reliable and effective forms of evidence. Observing physical inventory counts provides reliable evidence that the inventory actually exists. It may be more efficient to confirm the inventory held at the public warehouse but not as effective as observation. A, B, and C are not the most efficient means.

321. (C) I is correct. During a tour of the manufacturing plant or production facility, the auditor should be alert for items that appear to be old, obsolete, or defective. II is correct. Comparisons of inventory balances with anticipated sales volume might indicate higher inventory levels than would be expected, perhaps due to slow-moving, defective, or obsolete inventory items.

322. (C) I is correct. An auditor will make "test counts" of a client's inventory to be sure client count is accurate. II is correct. An auditor will make test counts of a client's inventory for later verification of final cost figures. In performing test counts, the auditor selects a sample of inventory items, counts them, and compares the result to the client's count.

323. (A) The auditor should test the client's physical inventory report by tracing test counts taken by the auditor to the client's physical inventory count report, thereby verifying the completeness of the client count. B is wrong. If the auditor began with the client's physical inventory listing and compared it to the auditor's test count, this would verify existence and test for overstatement of inventory. C is wrong. The auditor would test the rights and obligations assertion for inventory by reading loan agreements and the minutes of meetings to see if any inventory has been pledged. Also, inquiring if any inventory is here on consignment would relate to rights and obligations. D is wrong. The valuation assertion can be tested by touring the facility and performing analytical procedures regarding inventory turnover. Comparing inventory balances with anticipated sales volume might indicate higher inventory levels than would be expected, perhaps due to slow-moving, defective, or obsolete inventory.

324. (B) When the auditor begins with the client's physical inventory listing and compares it to the auditor's test count, this is to verify existence and test for overstatement of the client's inventory listing. Therefore, A, C, and D are wrong.

325. (B) II is correct. Starting with the tags and testing forward to the detailed inventory listing is a test for completeness. The auditor starts with what is believed to have happened—in this case, that inventory was counted—and moves to the event that is uncertain—that inventory was recorded. This is a test for understatement (completeness assertion). I is wrong. If the auditor began with the client's detailed inventory listing and moved to the tags, this would be a test for overstatement, or existence. In a good inventory count, the client would use prenumbered tags. This ensures that every item in the warehouse is counted because the client puts a physical tag on each item as it is counted. It also ensures that the client doesn't count something twice or count something that shouldn't be counted.

326. (A) I is correct. Tracing from inventory tags to the inventory listing schedule verifies the completeness of the schedule. II is wrong. Tracing from inventory tags to the inventory listing schedule verifies the completeness of the schedule, not the existence (or validity) of the items.

327. (A) I is correct. Tracing from the inventory schedule to the inventory tags and the auditor's record count sheets verifies the validity (existence) of the items. II is wrong. Tracing from the inventory schedule to the inventory tags and the auditor's record count sheets verifies the validity of the items, not the completeness of the schedule.

328. (A) I is correct. Tracing from receiving reports and vendors' invoices to the inventory listing are cutoff procedures used to verify completeness of the inventory listing. The auditor starts with the event that is believed to have taken place—that inventory was purchased and received—and moves to the event that is uncertain—that the inventory was recorded. II is wrong. For existence of the inventory, the auditor would begin with the inventory listing and move to see if there is support from a receiving report and vendor invoice. This would prove that the entries in the books for inventory are valid.

329. (B) As inventory gets older, the chance that its value will fall below cost goes up. As goods get older, they tend to get damaged or show other signs of age that may require them to be sold at a reduced price. Inventory is reported at the lower of cost or market. The increase in age might be a cause for the market value to decline so that a reduction in the reported balance will be necessary. A, C, and D are wrong. While presentation, existence, and completeness all pertain to inventory, the question asked about the age of the inventory.

330. (C) I is correct. Inventory purchased by Berman with terms FOB shipping point belongs to the buyer (Berman) while in transit. Therefore, this inventory should be counted at year-end even though it has not yet arrived. II is correct. Inventory shipped out on consignment by Berman still belongs to Berman until resold and should be counted at year-end.

331. (C) Verifying that all inventory owned by the client is on hand at the time of the count is not an objective when auditing inventories. Purchased items still in transit at year-end belong to the client under FOB shipping point. Items sold with terms FOB destination still belong to the seller (the client). Inventory out on consignment should also be included in inventory. Since certain items of inventory owned by the client are not on hand at year-end, the auditor would therefore not need to verify that all inventory owned is on hand. A is wrong. An auditor would gather evidence regarding appropriate presentation of inventory on the balance sheet. B is wrong. An auditor would gather evidence whether damaged goods and obsolete items have been properly accounted for. D is wrong. The auditor would gather evidence regarding inventory pricing and whether or not the inventory is priced using a method that is generally acceptable, such as LIFO or FIFO.

332. (B) II is correct. If purchases made before the end of the year have been recorded in the subsequent year, inventory will not be complete. The auditor uses cutoff tests to detect such situations and to determine that inventory quantities include all products owned by the company. (Note that the cutoff assertion is closely related to the completeness and occurrence assertions.) I is wrong. An auditor most likely would inspect loan agreements under which an entity's inventories are pledged to support the rights and obligations assertion for inventory.

333. (D) I is wrong. The disclosures involving inventory require inventory balances to be disclosed for work in process inventory. II is wrong. The disclosures involving inventory require inventory balances to be disclosed for raw materials. Under the category of presentation and disclosure, completeness is an assertion relating to inventory disclosure. For a manufacturer, disclosures related to inventory are required as follows: inventory balances for raw materials, work in process, and finished goods all need to be disclosed or the presentation and disclosure for inventory is not complete.

334. (A) I is correct. Assertions about accuracy deal with whether data related to recorded transactions have been included in the financial statements at appropriate amounts. II is wrong. Cutoff tests do not provide evidence related to the accuracy assertion for purchases, since accuracy assertion relates to what has been recorded, not what should have been recorded.

335. (B) I is correct. Inventories should be reduced, when appropriate, to replacement cost or net realizable value. This is closely related to the valuation of inventory. II is wrong. Understandability for inventory is related to inventory disclosures. III is wrong. Existence assertion for inventory relates to overstating inventory by counting inventory that does not exist.

336. (C) I is correct. Understandability and classification might be tested by confirming inventories pledged under loan agreements. The pledge or assignment of any inventory should be appropriately disclosed in the financial statements. II is correct. Understandability and classification might be tested by examining drafts of the financial statements for appropriate balance sheet classification.

Chapter 11: Audit Sampling

337. (A) I is correct. There are two types of statistical sampling: sampling for attributes and sampling for variables. Sampling for attributes involves sampling to determine whether controls are functioning as designed. The auditor relies on sampling for attributes when assessing control risk. II is wrong. Sampling for variables, not sampling for attributes, is concerned with evidence regarding account balances.

338. (C) I is correct. The first step in determining sample size for a test of controls is for the auditor to estimate the likely error rate in the population. II is correct. The second step in determining sample size for a test of controls is for the auditor to set a limit for how much error in the population the auditor could tolerate.

339. (C) When an auditor sampling for attributes, that is, testing controls, determines that the error rate is higher than originally expected, the sample size must be increased. A, B, and D are wrong.

340. (B) II is correct. The auditor fears that the sample will not be representative of the population as a whole. This risk is known as sampling risk or the allowable level of sampling risk. To lower that risk, the auditor needs to add more items to the sample. The larger the sample, the more likely it is to be representative of the population. I is wrong. To reduce sampling risk, the auditor will always have to sample a larger portion of the population.

341. (C) I is correct. The more errors expected in the population, the larger the sample size must be. When the auditor expects more errors, the auditor needs to be more careful and look at a larger sample. II is correct. The lower the level of sampling risk, the larger the sample size must be. If the auditor wants to reduce sampling risk from 10 percent to 5 percent, this means that the auditor wants to go from being 90 percent sure to being 95 percent sure that the sample represents the population. Anytime the auditor wants to be more certain that the sample represents the population, the sample size must be increased.

342. (A) I is correct. ~~The sample showed a 3 percent error rate,~~ but the population will always have a higher error rate than the sample. Given the parameters established by the auditor, the population error rate is calculated as 6.4 percent. The difference between the sample error rate and the upper deviation rate of the population is known as the allowance for sampling risk, 6.4 – 3 = 3.4. II is wrong. Since the upper deviation rate (new expected error rate of the population) is higher than the tolerable rate, the auditor would not find the control to be effective enough to lower the assessment of control risk.

343. (B) II is correct. The tolerable rate, given as 5 percent, is higher than the upper deviation rate, given as 4.4 percent. Therefore, the auditor will likely view the control as reliable and lower his or her assessment of control risk, thus leading to less substantive testing in this area of the audit. I is wrong. Although there were errors, the sample error rate of 3 percent translated into an upper deviation rate of 4.4 percent. Therefore, the auditor would not conclude that there were too many errors, since the upper deviation rate of 4.4 percent error was lower than the tolerable error rate of 5 percent.

344. (A) I is correct. The sample rate of deviation plus the allowance for sampling risk is equal to the upper deviation rate. The upper deviation rate is then compared to the tolerable deviation rate, and if the upper deviation rate is lower than the tolerable rate, the control is assessed as reliable. II is wrong. The tolerable deviation rate is equal to how much error the auditor can tolerate and still feel that the client's control is reliable. The auditor knows that some error is inevitable in any control or account balance. The tolerable deviation rate is set by the auditor.

345. (B) II is correct. Risk of assessing control risk too high relates to the efficiency of the audit. When control risk is assessed too high, more substantive procedures than needed will have to be performed, making the audit inefficient. I is wrong. As for effectiveness, if the substantive tests were done properly, the audit opinion should not be affected by the fact that the auditor assessed control risk too high. The audit will still be effective, just not particularly efficient.

346. (C) I is correct. To reduce sampling risk, the auditor will always have to sample a larger portion of the population. If the auditor selects more items, the chance that the sample will have characteristics different from the population goes down. II is correct. When sampling for variables, an auditor is estimating an account balance.

347. (A) I is correct. In every audit, there is a chance that a randomly chosen sample may not be representative of the population as a whole on the characteristic of interest. This concept is known as sampling risk. There will always be some element of sampling risk because an auditor does not examine 100 percent of the population. II is wrong. Selecting audit procedures that are not appropriate to achieve specific objectives relates to an error that could exist even if 100 percent of the population is examined (nonsampling risk). Audits are full of risk, both sampling risk as well as nonsampling risk.

348. (A) I is correct. The auditor knows that there will probably be some error in every account balance. Therefore, the auditor must set a limit for the largest amount of discovered error that can be tolerated before the account balance is considered not fairly presented. This is referred to as the tolerable error rate. II is wrong. If the auditor can tolerate a higher error rate, or if the auditor can tolerate a bigger misstatement in the client balance, the auditor will need to sample fewer items. The more problems that the auditor can tolerate the smaller the sample size can be.

349. (B) II is correct. The tolerable deviation rate is one of three parameters needed to determine sample size. The other two parameters are the expected error rate of the population and the allowable level of sampling risk. I is wrong. In attribute sampling, the number of items in the population is not a factor in determining sample size.

350. (C) I is correct. In variable sampling, which is done to test account balances, the number of items in the population is a significant factor in determining sample size. II is correct. In variable sampling, the allowable level of risk is an important parameter to determine sample size. The allowable level of risk refers to the risk that the auditor's sample has characteristics different from the population.

351. (C) Incorrect rejection of the account balance is where sample results support the conclusion that the recorded account balance was materially misstated when, in fact, it was not. The risk that a sample is not representative of the population is known as the allowable level of risk. When performing substantive tests, the allowable level of risk is the risk that the auditor makes the wrong conclusion regarding the account balance based on the sample. The question tells us that the sample was bad, as it made the account balance appear to be misstated when it was not. Therefore, the auditor would have incorrectly rejected the entire account balance as "not fairly presented," based on the sample. For those reasons, A, B, and D are wrong.

352. (D) Incorrect acceptance is when an auditor determines that the sample results support the conclusion that the recorded account balance is fairly presented, when in fact the account balance is materially misstated. The risk that a sample is not representative of the population is known as the allowable level of risk. When performing substantive tests, the allowable level of risk refers to the risk that the auditor makes the wrong conclusion regarding the account balance based on the sample. This question tells us that the sample made the account balance appear to be fairly presented when it was not. Therefore, the auditor would have incorrectly accepted the account balance. A, B, and C are wrong.

353. (D) Attribute sampling is used when testing controls. A, B, and C are wrong. PPS sampling and stratified sampling are variable sampling techniques that help the auditor deal with variability in a population. These methods would be common when the auditor is sampling to gather evidence for a client's accounts receivable.

354. (C) I is correct. One of the primary benefits of using generalized audit software is the ability to access client data stored in computer files without having a detailed understanding of the client's hardware and software features. II is correct. Generalized audit software allows an auditor to sample and test a much higher percentage of transactions, which results in a more reliable audit.

Chapter 12: Evidence Gathering and Transaction Cycles, Part 2

355. (A) I is correct. An auditor will confirm all client bank account balances. There is a standard bank confirmation form to expedite the process. The usefulness of the standard bank confirmation may be limited because the bank employee who completes the form may be unaware of all the financial relationships that the bank has with the client. II is wrong. The standard bank confirmation should request balances of all bank accounts, even those accounts that the client indicates were closed out during the year. The client may not have actually closed all of the accounts and may be using one to steal from the company.

356. (C) III is correct. Kiting involves the client's cash appearing as though it were in two bank accounts at the same time. To detect kiting, the auditor should review all checks and deposits clearing the bank two weeks after the end of the year. If found, these transactions should be scheduled to ensure that both the deposit and withdrawal are recorded in the correct time period. The auditor should request a bank cutoff statement from the bank for this purpose and prepare a bank transfer schedule. I is wrong. A bank reconciliation is a process that explains the difference between the bank balance shown in an organization's bank statement, as supplied by the bank, and the corresponding amount shown in the organization's own accounting records at a particular point in time. While an auditor would examine the client's bank reconciliation, it would not assist the auditor in detecting kiting. II is wrong. A bank cutoff statement is a statement obtained from the bank by the auditor that contains client deposits and checks that occurred 7 to 14 days after year-end. A bank cutoff statement is useful to gather evidence regarding whether or not deposits in transit at year-end actually cleared the bank. All deposits in transit that were listed on the year-end bank reconciliation should be listed on the bank cutoff statement. While the auditor would request a bank cutoff statement, it is not an auditor-prepared document.

357. (C) I is correct. The auditor should obtain bank cutoff statements that include transactions for 7 to 14 days after year-end. The outstanding checks at year-end on the bank reconciliation should have cleared the bank and be listed as a check on the bank cutoff statement. II is correct. The auditor should obtain bank cutoff statements that include transactions for 7 to 14 days after year-end. The deposits in transit at year-end on the bank reconciliation should have cleared the bank and be listed as a deposit in the bank cutoff statement.

358. (B) II is correct. Checks dated after year-end would not be included in the year-end outstanding check list. I is wrong. Checks dated after year-end might be on the bank cutoff statement. Some of those checks dated after year-end could have cleared the bank a week or two into the new year. When auditing cash, the auditor requests a bank cutoff statement to examine transactions that cleared a week or two into the new year.

359. (C) I is correct. A bank cutoff statement is used to verify the items appearing on a bank reconciliation. If theft has occurred, the fraud may be hidden by tampering with the information on the bank reconciliation. Therefore, the auditor should check the math on the reconciliation and verify all items that appear, such as the bank balance, deposits in transit, and outstanding checks. Information about each of these three items will be found in a bank cutoff statement. II is correct. If a deposit in transit is not recorded by the bank in a reasonable period of time, the auditor should be suspicious that the deposit was not really in transit. Likewise, if checks do not clear when anticipated, the auditor may be concerned that they were not actually outstanding at year's end.

360. (B) Municipal property tax bills prepared in the client's name are an example of external evidence that the client actually owns the property. If the question had asked about which assertion was affected by examining property tax bills, the rights and obligations assertion and existence assertion would be correct. A, C, and D are wrong.

361. (C) I is correct. A question about the existence of prenumbered purchase orders would likely be included on the internal control questionnaire since prenumbering functions are an important control supporting the completeness assertion. II is correct. A question about controls related to competitive bids would likely be included on a questionnaire related to controls over the initiation and execution of equipment purchases.

362. (B) II is correct. A debit to accumulated depreciation decreases the balance in that account. The retirement of plant assets necessitates the removal (decrease) of accumulated depreciation related to the retired asset by debiting accumulated depreciation. I is wrong. If the prior year's depreciation expense were understated (i.e., too low), the entry to correct the error would be a credit to accumulated depreciation.

363. (A) I is correct. Determining that proper amounts of depreciation are expensed provides assurance with regard to valuation and allocation related to the asset and assures accuracy in terms of financial statement presentation. II is wrong. Verifying depreciation computations does not provide evidence with respect to existence or occurrence.

364. (A) I is correct. Testing to see whether equipment listed in the accounting records is physically present in the plant and still in service is an effective way to test whether unrecorded disposals occurred. II is wrong. Reviewing whether depreciation is still being taken would not provide evidence about unrecorded fixed-asset disposals unless the auditor also performs a physical inspection of the assets being depreciated. Also, assets that are fully depreciated yet still in service would not appear in depreciation records.

365. (A) I is correct. The auditor should review the related repair and maintenance expense accounts to test for completeness of asset additions. The company may have recorded the payment but recorded it as an expense rather than an asset addition. The auditor is looking for items recorded as repairs that should have been capitalized, known as unrecorded additions. II is wrong. Testing to see whether equipment listed in the accounting records is physically still present in the plant and still in service is an effective way to test whether unrecorded disposals occurred but is not useful in finding unrecorded additions.

366. (B) II is correct. An analysis of depreciation expense would not identify fixed assets that were not properly capitalized, since no depreciation would be included for items not already classified as assets. I is wrong. An analysis of the repairs and maintenance account would best aid the auditor in verifying that all fixed assets have been capitalized. This account is generally analyzed to test for completeness of asset additions (i.e., the auditor is looking for items recorded as repairs or maintenance that would more properly have been capitalized as improvements of an asset).

367. (A) I is correct. To search for unrecorded disposals, the auditor would inspect the property ledger and the insurance and tax records, and then tour the client's facilities. II is wrong. Analysis of the repair and maintenance account is useful in identifying transactions that should have been capitalized versus expensed.

368. (D) I is wrong. Analyzing the repairs and maintenance account does not provide evidence about obsolete assets. The auditor reviews repair and maintenance expense accounts to test for completeness of asset additions. II is wrong. Analyzing the repairs and maintenance account does not provide evidence about the existence of assets. The auditor might select recorded plant and equipment assets and then physically locate and observe them in order to verify existence.

369. (D) I is wrong. Verifying depreciation computations does not provide evidence with respect to completeness but rather to valuation. II is wrong. Verifying depreciation computations does not provide evidence with respect to rights and obligations but rather to valuation.

370. (A) I is correct. Selecting items from the accounting records and attempting to locate them (existence) will reveal unrecorded retirements when the item cannot be located. II is wrong. Scanning the general journal for recorded entries is unlikely to reveal unrecorded retirements of equipment.

371. (A) I is correct. Accumulated depreciation is debited when an asset is sold. II is correct. The journal entry to retire an asset includes a debit to accumulated depreciation and a credit to the asset account. Accumulated depreciation is debited when an asset is retired. III is correct. Accumulated depreciation is debited when there is total and permanent impairment of an asset.

372. (A) I is correct. In most companies, long-term debt cannot be incurred without the formal approval of the board of directors. Therefore, evidence of the authorization of such debt should be sought to determine if all long-term liabilities are being reported by the company. II is wrong. A bank cutoff statement provides information about cash transactions in a checking account for 7 to 14 days after the end of the year and is unrelated to long-term debt. Rather than a bank cutoff statement, the auditor should review all bank confirmations for evidence of such debt balances as well as information on maturity dates, interest rates, and security agreements.

373. (B) I is correct. Contingencies often have little, if any, tangible documentation. A person, for example, simply may have made a threat against a company. Whenever physical evidence is lacking, the auditor will want to test the completeness assertion to ensure that no balances have been omitted. II is correct. With contingencies, the auditor should obtain evidence to support the valuation assertion. Uncertainty surrounds the outcome of any contingency so that the potential amount of loss may be difficult to assess, since it often involves anticipating the outcome of a court case. III is wrong. Existence relates to overstatement of liabilities, not understatement.

374. (D) I is correct. The reporting company should provide a listing of all contingencies. However, the auditor needs to ensure that other contingencies have not been omitted.

The auditor reads the minutes of the board of directors meetings for any discussions regarding contingent liabilities. II is correct. The reporting company should provide a listing of all contingencies. However, the auditor needs to ensure that other contingencies have not been omitted. The management rep letter gives the auditor an opportunity to inquire about contingencies. III is correct. Litigation surrounds many contingencies so that a review of the correspondence with the company's attorneys might bring discussion of contingencies to light.

375. (C) I is correct. Client contracts that contain a liquidated damages clause contain a contingent liability. A liquidated damages clause in a contract contains a specific dollar amount of damage, agreed to in advance, should that particular contract be breached. II is correct. Debt covenants contained in loan agreements sometimes allow the bank to call the loan due immediately in the event that the current ratio falls below a certain amount. For example, a typical debt covenant might allow the bank to call the client's loan due if the current ratio fell below 2:1. The auditor would read the bank confirmation letter because any debt covenant provides evidence of a contingent liability. The auditor would need to determine if a contingency exists at the balance sheet date from that particular loan being in breach of the debt covenant.

376. (C) I is correct. With regard to contingent losses, some method has to be derived to corroborate the company's assessment of the likelihood of each loss. II is correct. With regard to contingent losses, some method has to be derived to corroborate the estimated amount of each loss. Traditionally, the evidence regarding both the likelihood of each loss and the estimated amount has been obtained by sending a list of these contingencies, along with the possibility and amount of loss, to the company's attorneys, who are asked to indicate disagreements with that information. Attorneys need only provide information about cases in which they have had substantial participation. For those cases, disagreements should be indicated to the auditor. Otherwise, the attorney must state that sufficient knowledge is not available to render any type of assessment.

377. (B) I is correct. A primary objective when auditing liabilities is to determine that they are all properly included. Accordingly, the auditor has to search for liabilities that exist as of the balance sheet date. In searching for contingent liabilities, the auditor will typically review bank confirmation letters for any indication of direct or contingent liabilities. If the client's bank loan contained a debt covenant that required the current ratio to be 2:1 or better at all times, a direct or contingent liability would exist if the client were to fall below that ratio. III is correct. Examining invoices for professional services, especially from attorneys who may be working on pending litigation, may provide evidence of contingent liabilities. II is wrong. Accounts receivable confirmations provide evidence regarding assets, not liabilities.

378. (B) II is correct. If a claim has been omitted, in what's known as an unasserted claim, the lawyer should inform the client and suggest that the client disclose all details to the auditor. Information about unasserted claims must come from the client company. If that information is not subsequently conveyed by the client, the attorney should consider resigning. I is wrong. Information regarding unasserted claims would NOT come from the client's attorney. Information regarding unasserted claims would come from the client. Information regarding asserted (that is, not unasserted) claims would come from the client's attorney.

379. (C) The primary source of information to be reported about litigation, claims, and assessments is the client's management; the client's attorney is a secondary source. A is wrong. The client's attorney is the primary source of corroboration of evidence, but the primary source of evidence regarding litigation, claims, and assessments is the client. B is wrong. Court records are not a primary source of information. Court records would be a secondary rather than a primary source of evidence regarding litigation, claims, and assessments. D is wrong. The independent auditor is not a source of evidence regarding litigation, claims, and assessments. The independent auditor is searching for such evidence.

380. (D) The lawyer and the auditor should agree on materiality regarding litigation, claims, and assessments. A, B, and C are wrong. The client's management and governance should not get to decide what is material regarding such contingencies.

381. (C) I is correct. Unusual and large cash receipts, especially near the end of the year, should be investigated. The company could have recently borrowed the money and purposely not recorded the debt yet. II is correct. Reconciling interest expense to the reported amount of long-term debt is an analytical procedure useful in searching for understated liabilities. A very common analytical procedure is the anticipation of interest expense because the degree of reliability should be quite high; it is basically a mathematical calculation. If interest expense is higher than the auditor expects, the possibility arises that long-term debt has been omitted from the financial records. The interest is being paid but the debt is not being reported or is being understated, perhaps on purpose.

382. (A) I is correct. Analytical procedures and comparing auditor estimates to client actual amounts are required in the planning stage of an audit. II is wrong. Analytical procedures are not performed in the internal control stage. *Exam hint:* With an analytical procedures question, any answer choice that says "assess control risk" or "test controls" is the wrong answer because analytical procedures are not performed in the internal control stage.

383. (B) II is correct. In the overall review stage of the audit, analytical procedures are mandatory to search for any unusual relationships that would signify that more evidence gathering is needed. I is wrong. Analytical procedures are not required in the evidence-gathering stage but are optional. Sometimes analytical procedures can be performed as a substitute for a particular substantive test in the evidence-gathering stage.

384. (B) II is correct. A direct supervisor's approval of the time cards most effectively ensures that payment is paid for work performed, as the supervisor observes the employees and determines whether employees are present and working. I is wrong. Having employees record their arrival and departure by using the time clock does not ensure that the employees were actually present and/or working during the recorded time. Employees could clock in and then leave.

385. (A) I is correct. Segregation of duties between human resources and payroll departments is an important control to ensure that only valid employees receive paychecks. II is wrong. While all payroll checks should be printed in the payroll department, they are not signed in the human resources department but rather in the treasury department.

386. (B) I is correct. For effective internal control, the departmental supervisor should approve payroll and approve the hours that were worked prior to the payroll being processed. If the departmental supervisor distributed paychecks directly to departmental employees, then this would be incompatible functions, since the departmental supervisor would have access to assets (execution, distributing paychecks) and also authorization of the transaction (approval of payroll). The departmental supervisor could dismiss an employee and not notify human resources, keep the dismissed employee's paycheck, and forge an endorsement on the employee's check. III is correct. For effective internal controls, the pay rate should be established by the human resources department, not the employee's department supervisor. If the departmental supervisor set the pay rates, then he or she could be in collusion with the employee and obtain a kickback for paying an employee more than an established rate. II is wrong. For effective internal control, the departmental supervisor should approve payroll and approve the hours that were worked prior to the payroll being processed.

387. (A) I is correct. The occurrence assertion as it relates to payroll transactions would correspond to an audit objective to determine that payroll transactions actually occurred (i.e., that all payroll checks were issued to valid employees for hours actually worked). II is wrong. While an auditor would inspect prenumbered checks to see if any payroll checks were missing, inspecting evidence related to prenumbering of payroll checks would relate to the completeness assertion rather than existence or occurrence.

388. (C) Recomputing payroll deductions and verifying the preparation of the monthly payroll account bank reconciliation would provide significant evidence for the accuracy assertion for payroll transactions. A, B, and D are wrong. These assertions would not be supported by recomputing payroll deductions and verifying the preparation of the monthly payroll account bank reconciliation.

389. (D) I is wrong. Payroll checks generally are disbursed by the same person or the same department, a paymaster, each payday, and this would not cause the auditor to assess control risk as high or to suspect fraud. II is wrong. Time card approval by departmental supervisors is a standard practice and would not raise an auditor's suspicions of a payroll fraud scheme or assess control risk as high.

390. (C) Both I and II are correct. In assessing the work of the internal audit staff, competency and objectivity are the two primary criteria for making an evaluation.

391. (B) II is correct. The quality of the internal auditors' working paper documentation is likely to reflect their competence. I is wrong. Objectivity relates to how high up in the organization the internal audit staff report. The external auditor expects and hopes to see that the internal audit staff reports directly to the audit committee, and not to anyone within management, for maximum objectivity. No one in the organization should be able to intimidate the internal audit staff.

392. (D) Objectivity is reflected by the organizational level to which the internal auditor reports. A, B, and C relate to the competence of the internal auditor, but the question asks about the objectivity of the internal auditor.

393. (D) The internal auditor may assist the independent auditor in all three fieldwork standards: planning, internal control, and evidence gathering, usually in low-risk areas. The only areas of the audit where the internal auditor is excluded from any assistance are decisions requiring judgment and assessments.

394. (D) I is wrong. Assessing inherent risk requires an auditor's professional judgment, and while a competent and objective internal auditor may assist the independent auditor in all three fieldwork standards—planning, internal control, and evidence gathering—he or she may not participate in areas that require judgment. II is wrong for the same reason. Assessing control risk requires an auditor's professional judgment. While a competent and objective internal auditor may assist the independent auditor in all three fieldwork standards, he or she may not assist in areas that require judgment.

395. (D) I is wrong. Materiality levels require an auditor's professional judgment. The independent auditor may not subordinate his or her judgment to an internal auditor, even one who is competent and objective. II is wrong. Evaluating estimates made by management requires judgment. The independent auditor may not subordinate his or her judgment to an internal auditor, even one who is competent and objective.

396. (A) I is correct. The appropriateness and reasonableness of methods used are the responsibility of the specialist. II is wrong. While the appropriateness and reasonableness of methods used are the responsibility of the specialist, the auditor should obtain an understanding of the methods or assumptions used in order to determine whether the findings are suitable for corroborating the representations in the financial statements. However, the auditor is not required to perform substantive procedures to verify the specialist's assumptions and findings because the auditor, while highly trained in GAAS and GAAP, is often not capable of performing the same substantive tests that the specialist performed. If the auditor were able to perform those tests, there would have been no need for the specialist.

397. (D) I, II, and III are correct. When an independent auditor hires a specialist to perform certain substantive tests, an understanding should exist among the auditor, the client, and the specialist as to the nature of the work to be performed.

398. (D) I is wrong. When an independent auditor hires a specialist to perform certain substantive tests and believes that the specialist's findings are reasonable in the circumstances, the auditor would not mention the specialist in an unmodified opinion because the use of a specialist is quite common. II is wrong. When an independent auditor hires a specialist to perform certain substantive tests and believes that the specialist's findings are reasonable in the circumstances, the auditor may consider performing substantive procedures to verify the specialist's findings, especially if the specialist is somehow related to the client, but is not required to do so.

399. (A) I is correct. When an independent auditor hires a specialist to perform certain substantive tests and the auditor believes that the specialist's findings are contrary to the client's assertions, the auditor would mention the specialist in the auditor's report because the auditor's opinion would likely be affected. The auditor would mention the specialist in an emphasis paragraph. II is wrong. If the specialist were related to the client, the auditor may still be able to use that specialist, but the relationship would have an impact on the credibility of the findings.

Chapter 13: Ethics, Sarbanes-Oxley, and the COSO Framework

400. (C) Objectivity applies to all services rendered, but independence applies to attestation services only (audits, special reports, and reviews). Therefore, A, B, and D are wrong.

401. (D) I is correct. According to Rule 101 of the AICPA Code of Professional Conduct, independence will be impaired if a firm performs operational or financial decisions for clients. Performing one but not the other still impairs independence. II is correct. According to Rule 101, independence will be impaired if a firm performs management functions such as reporting to the board on behalf of management. III is wrong. Rule 101 also states that a firm may perform certain nonattest services for clients and still be independent as long as the firm does not serve or appear to serve as a member of the client's management.

402. (A) I is correct. The AICPA Code of Professional Conduct governs any service that a member of the AICPA performs. These services include audits, special reports, compilations, reviews, and services performed on financial forecasts and projections, as well as attestation engagements. II is wrong. Sarbanes-Oxley and its offspring, PCAOB, regulate publicly traded company audits and the firms that conduct those audits but do not replace the AICPA Code of Professional Conduct.

403. (C) The first three articles of the AICPA Code of Professional Conduct are: Article 1, Responsibilities; Article II, Public Interest; and Article III, Integrity. Article III, Integrity, states, "To maintain and broaden public confidence, members should perform all professional responsibilities with the highest sense of integrity." Integrity addresses the question of what is right and just. A and B are wrong. Article IV of the AICPA Code of Professional Conduct is titled Objectivity and Independence. D is wrong. Article V of the AICPA Code of Professional Conduct is titled Due Care.

404. (A) I is correct. A CPA must always be objective; however, a CPA need not be independent, except when engaged in public practice. According to the AICPA's code of conduct, "A member should maintain objectivity and be free of conflicts of interest in discharging professional responsibilities. A member in public practice should be independent in fact and appearance when providing auditing and other attestation services." II is wrong. A CPA need not be independent, except when engaged in public practice.

405. (A) I is correct. A state's society of CPAs is more of a social organization that promotes the profession through sponsored gatherings and committees and helps the CPA attain continuing education credits. It does NOT have the authority to revoke the CPA's license. II is correct. The AICPA is a standard-setting body that conducts hearings should a member violate the standards. If the member is found liable, the AICPA could recommend to the state board of accountancy that the CPA's license be suspended, but the AICPA has no power to revoke the CPA's license. III is wrong. The state board of accountancy has the power to revoke the CPA's license.

406. (B) II is correct. Issuing an unmodified opinion on the Year 12 financial statements when fees for the Year 11 audit were unpaid would be an ethics issue. Since fees are outstanding, a loan exists to the client. Auditors are not allowed to loan money to their clients. I is wrong. Most firms are sold for a percentage of fees collected over a multiple-year time frame. This would not be an ethics issue at all.

407. (B) II is correct. According to Rule 101, Independence, of the AICPA's code of conduct, a fully secured automobile loan with a financial institution client is permitted (regardless of the date obtained) and does not impair the independence rule. I is wrong. A home mortgage with an attestation client is not permitted; it would impair independence.

408. (B) II is correct. When a CPA leaves a firm and joins a client within one year of disassociating from the firm, independence will be impaired unless the engagement is reviewed by a qualified professional to determine whether the engagement team members maintained the appropriate level of skepticism when evaluating the representations and work of the former firm member. I is wrong. In this situation, independence is impaired unless the individual is no longer in a position to influence or participate in the firm's business.

409. (B) II is correct. Home mortgages given today to the auditor would impair the auditor's independence with respect to that lending institution. As this is a relatively new standard, home mortgages made before 2001 would not affect independence. I is wrong. Fully collateralized auto loans with financial institution clients are permissible and do not impair independence.

410. (D) Professional competence includes the technical qualifications of the CPA and of the CPA's staff, the ability to supervise and evaluate work, and the knowledge of technical subject matter or the ability to obtain that knowledge by research or by consulting with others.

411. (C) I is correct. The member must act as a reasonably prudent accountant would. II is correct. The CPA should exercise due professional care in the performance of professional services. The member must critically review work done by those assisting in the engagement at every level of supervision. The member must possess the same degree of skill commonly possessed by others in the field.

412. (A) I is correct. Contingent fees are specifically prohibited for audits and reviews of financial statements. II is correct. Contingent fees are specifically prohibited for examinations of prospective financial information. III is correct. A CPA is not allowed to have a fee contingent upon the size of a taxpayer's refund when filing an original tax return, Form 1040.

413. (B) II is correct. Contingent fees are permitted for compilations of financial statements expected to be used by third parties only if the member includes a statement that the member is not independent. III is correct. A contingent fee is permitted when representing a client in an examination of a tax return by an IRS agent. Note that a contingent fee is not allowed when preparing the client's original tax return. I is wrong. A contingent fee is not permissible with a review engagement or any engagement that requires independence.

414. (C) I is correct. False, misleading, or deceptive advertising is not allowed. II is correct. Advertising that is informative and objective is allowed.

415. (B) II is correct. Determination by a court or administrative agency of discrimination or harassment in public practice is considered an act discreditable to the profession. I is wrong. Work papers belong to the auditor. Failure to return work papers is not a problem; failure to retain client records would be an act discreditable to the profession. Failure to return client records after the client makes demand could result in loss of license.

416. (A) I is correct. Failure to retain client records would be an act discreditable to the profession under the AICPA Code of Professional Conduct. Failure to return client records after the client makes demand could result in loss of license even if the client has not yet paid the CPA's bill. If the CPA is still not paid after return of the client's original records, the CPA can seek legal or other collection remedies. II is wrong. A CPA may reveal confidential client information to a state CPA society quality review team. For a CPA to not reveal such information would require the CPA to cross out the client's name on every page and obliterate Social Security numbers, and this is not a requirement prior to sending financial statements and tax returns to the state review board for quality review purposes.

417. (D) I is wrong. Arranging with a collection agency to collect fees owed from clients does not violate the profession's ethical standards. II is wrong. There is no prohibition against using a cloud-based server to store confidential client files.

418. (D) III is correct. Independence is required for attestation engagements, audits, review engagements, examinations, or agreed-upon procedures. I is wrong. Compilations of personal financial statements do not require CPA independence. II is wrong. Compilations of financial forecasts do not require CPA independence. Compilations in general do not require independence, but if the CPA is not independent the report should so indicate.

419. (B) II is correct. Tax services may be provided to an issuer audit client but cannot include aggressive tax transactions with uncertain chances of success. I is wrong. Tax services may be provided to an issuer audit client but would need to be preapproved by the audit committee.

420. (D) I is wrong. The AICPA Code of Professional Conduct would NOT be violated if a member revealed confidential client information as a result of a validly issued subpoena or summons. A CPA must obey a court order. II is wrong. The AICPA Code of Professional Conduct would not be violated if a member revealed confidential client information as a result of a quality review of the CPA's practice. Quality review is still the standard for firm's not registered with PCAOB. For registered firms that audit publicly traded companies, PCAOB takes care of quality review.

421. (B) II is correct. According to the Sarbanes-Oxley Act of 2002, issuers must now be audited only by firms that register with PCAOB. I is wrong. Privately held companies can be audited by a CPA firm that is not registered with PCAOB even if the client does business with publicly traded companies.

422. (B) I is correct. PCAOB requires a registered CPA firm to provide a concurring or second partner review of each audit report. II is correct. PCAOB requires a registered CPA firm to describe in audit reports the scope of the testing of the issuer's internal control structure and procedures. III is wrong. PCAOB requires a registered CPA firm to maintain audit documentation for seven years. Criminal penalties will apply for failure to retain work papers for at least seven years.

423. (C) I is correct. Audit firms need to retain work papers relating to their audit clients for at least seven years if the client is publicly held. II is correct. Audit firms need to retain work papers relating to their audit clients for at least five years if the client is not publicly held.

424. (C) I is correct. Registered firms must report to the audit committees of audited corporations any material written communications between the audit firm and management, including a schedule of unadjusted audit differences. II is correct. Registered firms must report to the audit committee's alternative accounting treatments discussed with the corporation's management, the ramifications of the alternatives, and the treatment the firm prefers.

425. (A) A cooling-off period of one year is required before a former member of an audit client engagement team can be employed in a financial oversight role for that same client. This requirement is necessary to preserve auditor (firm) independence. This is to reduce the chance of a conflict of interest.

426. (C) I is correct. According to Sarbanes-Oxley, the lead auditor or coordinating partner auditing a publicly traded company must rotate off the audit every five years. II is correct. According to Sarbanes-Oxley, the reviewing partner involved in a publicly traded audit engagement must rotate off the audit every five years. Under PCAOB, these individuals must take a time-out of five years before returning to that same audit client.

427. (D) I is wrong. The AICPA Code of Professional Conduct, which is followed when auditing nonissuers, does not require audit partner rotation. II is wrong. The PCAOB/SEC ethical standards that apply to the audits of issuers require that the lead partner rotate off the audit engagement after five years. PCAOB does not apply to the audit of a nonissuer.

428. (A) I is correct. According to Title VI of Sarbanes-Oxley, any officer, director, or owner of more than 10 percent of any equity security must file a report indicating how many shares he or she owns within 10 days after becoming an officer, director, or more than 10 percent owner. II is wrong. According to Title VI of Sarbanes-Oxley, any officer, director, or owner of more than 10 percent of any equity security must file a report of change in ownership within two days of such change.

429. (C) I is correct. According to Sarbanes-Oxley, auditors are required to attest to management's assessment of the effectiveness of internal control over financial reporting in a 10-K Annual Report. Form 10-K must include an internal control report stating management's responsibility for establishing an adequate internal control structure and procedure for financial reporting and an assessment of the effectiveness of the current year's control structure.

II is correct. According to Sarbanes-Oxley, auditors are required to attest to management's assessment of the effectiveness of internal control over financial reporting in a 10-Q Quarterly Report. Form 10-Q must include an internal control report stating management's responsibility for establishing an adequate internal control structure and procedure for financial reporting and an assessment of the effectiveness of the current year's control structure. Auditors are required to attest to management's assessment of the effectiveness of internal control over financial reporting.

430. (A) I is correct. Firms registered with PCAOB are required to undergo PCAOB inspection. These inspections occur every three years or every year depending on how many publicly traded company audits are conducted by the firm. If the firm audits more than 100 publicly traded companies annually, PCAOB will inspect that firm every year. Otherwise, these inspections will occur every three years. II is wrong. Firms registered with PCAOB are required to undergo PCAOB inspection, not peer review. Peer review is for the firms not registered with PCAOB. Peer review evidently wasn't doing a good enough job inspecting the large firms prior to the accounting scandals that led up to the Sarbanes-Oxley Act of 2002. PCAOB has replaced peer review for the large firms.

431. (D) I is wrong. Sarbanes-Oxley does NOT require rotation of the issuer's designated financial expert every five years. II is wrong. Sarbanes-Oxley does NOT require rotation of the issuer's auditing firm every five years. The issuer does not have to change audit firms, but the audit firm has to rotate lead partners every five years.

432. (C) I is correct. The SEC requires each issuer to disclose in Forms 10-K and 10-Q whether or not they have an audit committee financial expert. If they do not have an audit committee financial expert, they must state their reasons why. II is correct. The SEC requires each issuer to disclose in Forms 10-K and 10-Q whether or not the entity has a code of ethics for senior financial officers. If there is no code, the entity must state its reasons why.

433. (B) Any other partner, principal, shareholder, or managerial employee of the firm who provided 10 or more hours of nonaudit services to the audit client or expects to provide 10 or more hours of nonaudit services to the client on a recurring basis is no longer independent. The same is true for any other partner, principal, or shareholder from an office of the accounting firm in which the lead audit engagement partner primarily practices in connection with the audit. Therefore, A, C, and D are wrong.

434. (C) Under Sarbanes-Oxley, lead partners and concurring partners are subject to a five-year "time-out" period before returning to an engagement. Other audit partners are subject to a two-year time-out period. These rules apply to audits of publicly traded companies. Rotation and time out are not required for audits of nonissuers.

435. (B) II is correct. For audits of issuers, assisting the client in aggressive tax transactions would be a violation of independence. I is wrong. For audits of nonissuers, assisting the client in aggressive tax transactions would NOT be a violation of independence.

436. (C) Both I and II are correct. Under both Sarbanes-Oxley and AICPA standards, auditor independence is impaired if any of the following nonaudit services are provided during the audit or during the professional engagement period: bookkeeping or other services related to the accounting records or financial statements of the audit client; financial information systems design and implementation; appraisal or valuation services; and actuarial services.

437. (A) I is correct. According to Sarbanes-Oxley, accounting firms that audit publicly traded companies cannot perform certain services for those companies. Among the prohibited services are bookkeeping services. II is wrong. While many nonaudit services for an audit client are now prohibited under Sarbanes-Oxley, income tax return preparation is still allowed.

438. (B) II is correct. If the audit committee doesn't designate a member as the financial expert on the audit committee, the audit process still goes on but the reason for lack of financial expert must be disclosed. I is wrong. Sarbanes-Oxley does not require that the audit committee chairperson be its financial expert.

439. (A) I is correct. Among the powers of PCAOB is the ability to discipline the members of the profession involved with violations while auditing publicly traded companies. PCAOB can reprimand, fine, or suspend a member or member firm from auditing public companies. II is wrong. Accounting standards come from the Financial Accounting Standards Board (FASB). Auditing, quality control, and independence standards come from PCAOB.

440. (D) Nonaudit services that do not exceed 5 percent of total revenues from an audit client do not require audit committee preapproval as long as the services are brought to the audit committee's attention and approved before the completion of the audit. The general rule is that all services must be preapproved by the audit committee. This would include tax services and other nonaudit services, even those performed on a recurring basis.

441. (B) The internal control provisions of Sarbanes-Oxley apply to public companies only. Sarbanes-Oxley does not apply to private companies. Therefore, A, C, and D are wrong.

442. (C) I is correct. Sarbanes-Oxley requires a publicly traded company to report on its own internal control. II is correct. Sarbanes-Oxley requires a publicly traded company to make an assertion regarding the effectiveness of its own internal control. This report must include a statement by management taking responsibility for the internal control and identifying the framework for evaluating the internal control.

443. (B) Sarbanes-Oxley requires a publicly traded company to report on its own internal control and make an assertion regarding the effectiveness of its own internal control. This report must include a statement by management taking responsibility for the internal control and identifying the framework for evaluating the internal control. The most common management tool for evaluating internal control is the COSO internal framework. The COSO framework of evaluating internal control is recognized as appropriate by both the

SEC and PCAOB. Management simply mentions this framework in its report on internal control. A, C, and D are wrong.

444. (D) According to the COSO internal framework for evaluating internal control, the five components of internal control are (1) control environment, (2) risk assessment, (3) control activities, (4) information and communication, and (5) monitoring.

445. (C) Both I and II are correct. The COSO framework of evaluating internal control is recognized as appropriate by both PCAOB and the SEC. Management simply mentions COSO as the framework in its report on internal control.

446. (C) I is correct. In management's report on internal control (required under Sarbanes-Oxley for publicly traded companies), another component of the report is a statement that the company's independent auditor has issued an attestation report on management's assertion. II is correct. In management's report on internal control, management mentions COSO as the framework for reporting and evaluating its internal control.

447. (D) I is correct. Management's report on internal control for a publicly traded company must include a statement that management is responsible for internal control. II is correct. Management's report on internal control for a publicly traded company must include a statement that the "independent auditor has assessed management's assertion" regarding internal control. III is correct. Management's report on internal control for a publicly traded company must also include management's assertion regarding the effectiveness of the company's internal control.

448. (C) Both I and II are correct. The five interrelated components of internal control, according to the COSO framework, are (1) control environment, (2) risk assessment, (3) control activities, (4) information and communication, and (5) monitoring.

449. (D) Note that the question asks which are NOT part of the COSO framework. The other three components of the COSO framework are control environment, information and communication, and monitoring.

450. (A) I is correct. The auditor must report to those charged with governance all significant deficiencies. Significant deficiencies are those control deficiencies that are discovered by the auditor and that the auditor considered significant enough to report. III is correct. The auditor must report to those charged with governance all material weaknesses. Material weaknesses are more severe than significant deficiencies. A material weakness can be a combination of significant deficiencies. II is wrong. Control deficiencies may be reported but are not required unless they are significant deficiencies or material weaknesses.

451. (D) An auditor must communicate material weaknesses and significant deficiencies to those charged with governance. The timing is up to the auditor, so the communication could be done during the audit or at the audit's completion.

Chapter 14: International Auditing Standards, Government Auditing Standards, and Information Technology

452. (C) According to the IFAC, marketing of professional services is allowed if the content of the marketing promotion is honest and truthful. A and D are wrong because no particular form of marketing is prohibited. B is wrong because marketing must be honest and truthful as well as legal.

453. (B) The international code of ethics for professional accountants has fewer outright prohibitions than the AICPA Code of Professional Conduct. For example, international standards do NOT outright prohibit internal audit outsourcing, actuarial services, and financial information system design and implementation. While the AICPA Code of Professional Conduct and Sarbanes-Oxley consider those nonaudit services to be a violation of independence, IFAC permits such services if appropriate safeguards exist. D is wrong because the IFAC code of ethics applies to all professional accountants.

454. (B) II is correct. While PCAOB generally requires external confirmations of accounts receivable, international standards do NOT require external confirmations of receivables. I is wrong. Per international standards, the location in which the auditor practices must be disclosed in the audit report.

455. (B) II is correct. Under international standards, if the client suddenly wishes to change the engagement and the auditor is unable to agree with the client as to the reason for the sudden change, the auditor should withdraw and consider whether there is an obligation to contact third parties. I is wrong. Under international audit standards, dual dating is not allowed. When dating the audit report for a subsequent event, international standards require the dating of the report to be the amended date.

456. (B) II is correct. IFRS are the international accounting standards. They represent an alternative to US GAAP. I is wrong. IFRS are the international accounting standards, NOT the international auditing standards. IFRS are developed by the International Accounting Standards Board. Since IFRS are not auditing standards, IFRS are not an alternative to PCAOB.

457. (A) I is correct. United States auditors will sometimes report on financial statements of a US entity that have been prepared in conformity with another country's accounting principles. The auditor can issue an unmodified opinion or any other opinion, but first the auditor needs to understand the accounting principles generally accepted in the foreign country. II is wrong. There is no need for the auditor to be certified in the foreign country. It is enough to have an understanding of the accounting principles used in that country.

458. (D) I is wrong. Internal audit outsourcing services may not be provided to audit clients under US ethics standards. II is wrong. Under IFAC's code of ethics, an auditor may provide internal audit services if appropriate safeguards are put in place to limit or eliminate any threats to independence.

459. (D) I, II, and III are correct. Government Auditing Standards define three types of engagements: financial audits, attest engagements, and performance audits.

460. (C) I is correct. In a compliance audit, the auditor reports on whether the entity has complied with applicable requirements. II is correct. In a compliance audit the auditor does not express an opinion on the effectiveness of internal control over compliance.

461. (C) I is correct. In performing an audit in accordance with Generally Accepted Government Auditing Standards (the "Yellow Book"), the auditor accepts greater reporting responsibilities than accepted under a GAAS audit, since the auditor must report on compliance with laws, rules, and regulations, violations of which may affect financial statement amounts. II is correct. In performing an audit in accordance with Generally Accepted Government Auditing Standards, the auditor must report on the organization's internal control over financial reporting.

462. (A) I is correct. Compared to a typical GAAS audit, a government audit entails expanded internal control and testing requirements. A government audit involves a formal written report on the consideration of internal control and assessment of control risk. II is wrong. Compared to a typical GAAS audit, government audits require expanded reporting to include whether the federal financial assistance has been administered in accordance with laws and regulations.

463. (C) I is correct. Per Government Auditing Standards, audit documentation should contain sufficient information so that supplementary oral explanations are not required. II is correct. Assessed risk of material noncompliance must be documented, including procedures performed and understanding of internal control. This can be in the form of a flowchart, questionnaire, or narrative, but it must be documented.

464. (B) II is correct. An objective of a compliance audit of a governmental entity is to form an opinion on whether that government complied with applicable compliance requirements in all material respects. I is wrong. The auditor cannot minimize control risk of noncompliance, since control risk exists independently of the audit. The auditor can only assess control risk of noncompliance.

465. (C) I is correct. Auditors engaged to perform a single audit must perform procedures to obtain an understanding of internal control pertaining to the compliance requirements for federal programs sufficient to plan an audit. II is correct. Auditors engaged to perform a single audit must perform procedures to support a low assessed level of control risk for major programs. Testing controls is the way to support a low assessed level of control risk.

466. (A) I is correct. Auditors engaged to perform a single audit must perform procedures to obtain an understanding of internal control pertaining to the compliance requirements for federal programs sufficient to plan an audit and to support a low assessed level of control risk for programs considered to be major programs. II is wrong. Auditors have NO responsibility to obtain an understanding of internal control over compliance or perform related tests of compliance for any federal program deemed to be nonmajor.

467. (C) I is correct. Under the Single Audit Act, auditors are responsible for understanding internal control. The auditor must understand internal control over financial reporting and over federal programs sufficient to plan the audit to support a low assessed level of control risk for major programs. II is correct. Under the Single Audit Act, auditors are responsible for reporting the results of their tests. Significant deficiencies and material weaknesses must be disclosed.

468. (A) I is correct. GAGAS require a written report on the auditor's understanding of internal control and the assessment of control risk in all audits. II is wrong. GAAS require written communication only when significant deficiencies are noted. Significant deficiencies should be reported to specific legislative and regulatory bodies.

469. (C) I is correct. When compared to GAAS audits, reporting responsibilities under GAGAS are expanded to include reports on compliance with laws, rules, and regulations, violations of which may affect financial statement amounts. II is correct. Responsibilities under GAGAS include reports on internal control over financial reporting.

470. (C) I is correct. Program-specific audits do NOT include reports on the financial statements of the organization taken as a whole. Under certain circumstances, recipients of federal monies are allowed to have program-specific audits rather than a full single audit. II is correct. The Single Audit Act allows an entity that spends more than $500,000 per year to have an audit of each specific program rather than a single audit, but only if criteria are met.

471. (C) A single audit represents a combined audit of both an entity's financial statements and its federal financial assistance programs. The single audit provides audited organizations with the opportunity to capitalize on the efficiency of satisfying their audit requirements with a single audit. Auditors are governed by the Single Audit Act and OMB Circular A-133.

472. (B) II is correct. Continuous performance of tests of controls is required when financial data are processed electronically, without provision of paper documentation, to ensure that controls are operating effectively throughout the period under audit. I is wrong. Consideration of the risk of management fraud is required in all audits, regardless of the method used to process financial data or the adequacy of the paper documentation provided.

473. (A) III is correct. The audit program will likely need to be revised to reflect the risks and capitalize on the strengths inherent in an automated system. For example, there will likely be a greater risk of unauthorized access, while there may also be greater opportunities for data analysis and review. I is wrong. If specialized IT skills are needed, the auditor is less likely to take IT courses and more likely to seek the assistance of an IT professional. II is wrong. Audit objectives are the same in a computerized environment as they are in a manual environment. The audit procedures to accomplish those objectives may need to change, but the objectives are the same.

474. (C) I is correct. Using test data, an auditor is likely to test a request for two checks for the same employee, and the computer would be expected to print an error report. If the client's payroll program printed out two checks for the same employee, the auditor would assess control risk as high for payroll. II is correct. A request for a check to be paid to an employee who no longer works for the company should result in an error report. If the client's payroll program prints out the payroll check for the terminated employee, the auditor would assess control risk as high for payroll.

475. (B) II is correct. Integrated test facility (ITF) allows dummy transactions to be run simultaneously with live transactions in the client's computer system. ITF is often programmed into the computer for this purpose. I is wrong. Test data are a set of dummy transactions developed by the auditor and processed through the client's computer system but not at the same time that the client is using the computer for live transactions. Test data sometimes are performed by default because ITF was not programmed into the system.

476. (B) II is correct. Parallel simulation is a computer-assisted audit technique that permits an auditor to insert the auditor's version of a client's program to process data and compare the output with the client's output. I is wrong. Test data are a set of dummy transactions developed by the auditor and processed through the client's computer system but not at the same time that the client is using the computer for live transactions.

477. (B) I is correct. Generalized audit software would be used when constructing parallel simulations. Parallel simulation involves taking the client's data and reprocessing that data using the auditor's equipment and software. III is correct. The auditor would use generalized audit software or retrieval package software to access client data files. II is wrong. The assessment of control risk is based on auditor judgment. A computer cannot replace auditor professional judgment in assessing IT control risk.

Chapter 15: Management Representation Letter and Quality Control at the Firm

478. (A) I is correct. The management rep letter is considered the final piece of audit evidence and, under both US GAAS and PCAOB standards, must be dated the same as the audit report. II is wrong. The management rep letter is a required piece of audit evidence. An auditor's failure to receive a signed rep letter would result in a scope limitation likely to result in a disclaimer or a withdrawal from the engagement.

479. (C) I is correct. The CEO would be asked to sign the management rep letter because the CEO has control over operations. II is correct. The CFO would be asked to sign the rep letter because the CFO has control over financial matters. Note that members of management with responsibility over financial and operating matters would ordinarily sign the rep letter, and other officers may also be asked to sign the rep letter.

480. (D) I is wrong. Materiality does not apply to the level of access that management has given to the auditor regarding access to minutes of board meetings. Either the auditor was given access or he or she wasn't. II is wrong. Materiality does not apply to the level of access that management has given to the auditor regarding records relating to revenue and expenses. Once again, either the auditor was given access or he or she wasn't. In a management representation letter, materiality may or may not apply, and often it doesn't.

481. (A) I is correct. In a typical management representation letter, management would acknowledge its responsibility for fair presentation of financial statements. II is correct. In a typical management representation letter, management would acknowledge its responsibility for internal control over financial reporting. III is wrong. In a typical management representation letter, management would NOT acknowledge its responsibility for communications with the audit committee. The management rep letter deals with communications between management and the auditor, not communications between management and the audit committee.

482. (C) I is correct. In the management rep letter, management should disclose the results of its assessment of the risk that the financial statements may be materially misstated due to fraud. II is correct. In the management rep letter, management should acknowledge that all known or potential litigation has been disclosed to the auditor and accounted for and dis closed in the financial statements or footnotes in accordance with the applicable framework.

483. (A) A statement such as "There are no material transactions that have not been prop- erly recorded in the accounting records underlying the financial statements" most likely would be found in the management rep letter, which is stored in the current file. In the management rep letter, management acknowledges that the financial statements are com- plete and that all material transactions have been recorded. B is wrong. This excerpt would NOT be found in the communication with the predecessor. The first communication with the predecessor, prior to the engagement acceptance, would be concerned with the integrity of the client. A second, optional communication with the predecessor after the engagement has been accepted would be concerned with the client's opening balances. C is wrong. The engagement letter would be concerned with the responsibilities of management and respon- sibilities of the auditor. Further, the auditor never makes such a statement. D is wrong. This excerpt would not appear in the auditor's report. The auditor never makes such a statement. Instead, the auditor provides an opinion as to fair presentation of the financial statements in accordance with the framework.

484. (C) The statement "Fees for our services are based on our per diem rates plus travel expenses" would be most likely found in the engagement letter. In the engagement letter, the auditor includes a section on fees and frequency of billing. The engagement letter is stored in the current file. A is wrong. This excerpt would NOT be found in the auditor's report. The auditor's report does not mention fees charged to the client by the auditor. B is wrong. This excerpt would NOT be found in the audit inquiry letter to legal counsel. The auditor's letter to legal counsel asks the client's lawyer to respond to questions regarding contingent liabilities. D is wrong. This passage would NOT be found in the management rep letter, as fees for the audit are not mentioned in the management rep letter. The man- agement representation letter is where management acknowledges in writing its answers to various inquiries from the auditor.

485. (A) The excerpt "The objective of our audit is to express an opinion on the financial statements, although it is possible that facts or circumstances encountered may prevent us from expressing an unmodified opinion" would most likely be found in the auditor's engagement letter. The engagement letter contains a section regarding limitations of the engagement. The fact that there are potential limitations to being able to express any opin- ion should be mentioned in the engagement letter. The engagement letter is stored in the current file. B is wrong. This passage would NOT be found in the management rep letter. The management representation letter is where management acknowledges in writing its answers to various inquiries from the auditor. C is wrong. This passage would NOT be found in the auditor's inquiry to client's legal counsel. The auditor's letter to legal counsel asks the client's lawyer to respond to questions regarding contingent liabilities. D is wrong. This passage would NOT be found in the auditor's communication with the predecessor.

The auditor's communication prior to the engagement acceptance would be concerned with the integrity of the client. A second, optional communication with the predecessor after the engagement has been accepted would be concerned with the client's opening balances.

486. (C) The excerpt "There has been no fraud involving employees that could have a material effect on the financial statements" would be found in the management rep letter. In the rep letter at the end of the audit, the auditor asks the client to acknowledge that there has been no fraud involving employees that could have a material effect on the financial statements. The management rep letter is stored in the current file. A is wrong. This statement would NOT be found in the auditor's communication with the audit committee. The auditor's communication with the audit committee might include instances of fraud observed or even suspected. B is wrong. This statement would NOT be found in the audit inquiry letter to legal counsel. The auditor's letter to legal counsel asks the client's lawyer to respond to questions regarding contingent liabilities. D is wrong. This statement would NOT be found in the audit communication with the predecessor auditor. The auditor's communication prior to the engagement acceptance would be concerned with the integrity of the client. A second, optional communication with the predecessor after the engagement has been accepted would be concerned with the client's opening balances.

487. (D) The passage "Are you aware of any facts or circumstances that may indicate a lack of integrity by any member of senior management?" would likely appear in the auditor's communication with the predecessor auditor. The successor would want to know about any issues that would indicate that management of the potential new audit client lacks integrity. The communication with the predecessor would be stored in the current file. A is wrong. This passage would NOT be contained in the management rep letter. The management rep letter is where management acknowledges in writing its answers to various inquiries from the auditor. B is wrong. This passage would NOT be contained in the engagement letter. The engagement letter sets forth the agreement between the auditor and the client. The auditor would not ask the client about management integrity but would instead ask the predecessor auditor. C is wrong. This passage would NOT be contained in the auditor's report. The auditor's report provides an opinion as to fair presentation of the financial statements in accordance with the framework.

488. (C) The excerpt "There were unreasonable delays by management in permitting the start of the audit and in providing needed information" would likely be found in the auditor's communication with the audit committee. The auditor would indicate these delays to the audit committee in receiving requested information. This communication with the audit committee would be stored in the current file. A is wrong. The passage would NOT be found in an accounts receivable confirmation. In an accounts receivable confirmation (now called an external confirmation), the auditor asks the client's customers for information about the balances owed to the client. B is wrong. The passage would NOT be found in the auditor's engagement letter. The engagement letter is between the client and the auditor, not between the auditor and the audit committee. D is wrong. The passage would NOT be found in the management rep letter. The rep letter includes statements made by management to the auditor, not statements made by the auditor to the audit committee.

489. (A) The excerpt "If this statement is not correct, please write promptly, using the enclosed envelope, and give details of any differences directly to our auditors" is most likely taken from an accounts receivable confirmation. In an accounts receivable confirmation (now called an external confirmation), the auditor asks the client's customers for information about the balances owed to the client. These responses should mailed back to the auditor directly, without client interference, and the auditor should store these responses in the current file. B is wrong. This statement would NOT be found in the management rep letter. The management rep letter includes statements made by management to the auditor, not evidence involving the client's customers. C is wrong. This statement would NOT be found in the audit inquiry to legal counsel. The auditor's letter to legal counsel asks the client's lawyer to respond to questions regarding contingent liabilities, not about balances owed to the client from customers. D is wrong. This statement would NOT be found in the auditor's communication with the predecessor. The auditor's communication with the predecessor prior to engagement acceptance would be concerned with the integrity of the client. A second, optional communication with the predecessor after the engagement has been accepted would be concerned with the client's opening balances. The auditor's communication with the predecessor is not concerned with specific customer balances owed to the client.

490. (D) The excerpt "The company has suffered recurring losses from operations and has a net capital deficiency that raises substantial doubt about its ability to continue as a going concern" would most likely be found in the auditor's report. In the auditor's report, the auditor would include an emphasis-of-matter paragraph, after the opinion paragraph, to describe any matter that the auditor wanted to call to the user's attention. Going concern would be an example of an issue that would receive such an emphasis paragraph. The auditor's report could still be unmodified even with the emphasis-of-matter paragraph. The auditor's report would be stored in the current file. A is wrong. This passage would NOT be found in the audit inquiry letter to legal counsel. The auditor's letter to legal counsel asks the client's lawyer to respond to questions regarding contingent liabilities. B is wrong. The passage would NOT be found in accounts receivable confirmations. In an accounts receivable confirmation (now called an external confirmation), the auditor asks the client's customers for information about the balances owed to the client. It would not mention recurring losses. C is wrong. This statement would NOT be found in the auditor's communication with the predecessor. The auditor's communication with the predecessor prior to engagement acceptance would be concerned with the integrity of the client. A second, optional communication with the predecessor after the engagement has been accepted would be concerned with the client's opening balances. Going concern has to do with the client's ending balances.

491. (A) I is correct. The AICPA Code of Professional Conduct requires firms providing auditing, attestation, and accounting and review services to adopt a system of quality control. A quality control system consists of policies and procedures designed, implemented, and maintained to ensure that the firm complies with professional standards and also ensures that the reports that are issued by the firm are appropriate in the circumstances. II is wrong. The Internal Revenue Service does NOT require audit firms to adopt a system of quality control.

492. (B) The human resources element of quality control (at the firm) deals with recruitment and hiring practices, assigning personnel to engagements, professional development, performance evaluation, compensation, and advancement. A is wrong. A CPA firm's leadership responsibilities for quality within the firm are essential because a firm's leadership bears the ultimate responsibility for the firm's quality control systems. The tone at the top of a firm influences attitudes throughout the firm. C is wrong. Risk assessment is NOT an element of quality control at the firm. D is wrong. Monitoring helps the firm determine whether the quality control system has been designed appropriately and implemented effectively.

493. (A) Considering audit risk is NOT an element of quality control at the firm. The elements of quality control at the firm are:

Client acceptance and continuance
Human resources
Ethical requirements
Leadership
Monitoring
Performance

494. (A) I is correct. A CPA firm's leadership responsibilities for quality within the firm are essential because a firm's leadership bears the ultimate responsibility for the firm's quality control systems. The tone at the top of a firm influences attitudes throughout the firm. II is wrong. While performing the engagement within its reporting deadlines is essential, it falls under the quality control category known as client acceptance and continuance.

495. (A) When measuring the quality control at a CPA firm, providing a means to resolve differences of opinion falls under the category of performance. A firm should strive to achieve a consistently high level of performance. All audit work should be supervised and appropriately reviewed. Experts may need to be consulted for complex and unusual issues. B is wrong. Leadership relates to a CPA firm's tone at the top. The tone at the top of a firm influences attitudes throughout the firm. C is wrong. Monitoring helps the firm determine whether the quality control system has been designed appropriately and implemented effectively. D is wrong. The human resources element of quality control (at the firm) deals with recruitment and hiring practices, assigning personnel to engagements, professional development, performance evaluation, compensation, and advancement.

496. (C) Monitoring helps the firm determine whether the quality control system has been designed appropriately and implemented effectively. A is wrong. Performance relates to the idea that all audit work should be supervised and appropriately reviewed. Experts may need to be consulted for complex and unusual issues. B is wrong. Leadership relates to a CPA firm's tone at the top. The tone at the top of a firm influences attitudes throughout the firm. D is wrong. The human resources element of quality control (at the firm) deals with recruitment and hiring practices, assigning personnel to engagements, professional development, performance evaluation, compensation, and advancement.

497. (B) II is correct. Sarbanes-Oxley requires in every public company audit a "wrap-up" or secondary partner review of the audit documentation by a partner not otherwise involved in the audit. The primary purpose of this second partner review is to ensure that the financial statements are presented in accordance with the framework. I is wrong. Peer review is an attempt at self-regulation as one firm reviews another. The purpose of peer review is to determine whether the CPA firm being reviewed has developed adequate policies and procedures for the elements of quality control and is following them in practice. While firms that are members of the AICPA get peer reviewed every three years, Sarbanes-Oxley ended self-regulation for firms that audit public companies. PCAOB now regulates the larger audit firms, and those firms are no longer peer reviewed.

498. (C) I is correct. A firm that fails to maintain quality control standards has NOT necessarily violated generally accepted auditing standards. Quality control standards relate to the conduct of a firm's entire practice, whereas professional standards such as GAAS relate to the conduct of an individual engagement. II is correct. While the adoption of quality control standards does increase the likelihood of compliance with professional standards on individual engagements, quality control standards relate to the conduct of a firm's entire practice, whereas professional standards such as GAAS relate to the conduct of an individual engagement.

499. (B) II is correct. The CPA firm's size and cost-benefit considerations should be taken into account with regard to the nature and extent of the firm's quality-control policies and procedures. I is wrong. The CPA firm's size and cost-benefit considerations have nothing to do with independence.

500. (B) II is correct. Quality-control policies and procedures should provide the CPA firm with reasonable assurance that the likelihood of associating with clients whose management lacks integrity is minimized. Within quality-control standards is a component dedicated to engagement acceptance and continuance. I is wrong. Quality-control standards apply to auditing and attestation as well as accounting and review services.

Bonus Questions

501. (B) II is correct. Under IFAC, a two-year time-out is appropriate for lead partners, while under PCAOB standards, the time-out for lead partners is five years after they have been rotated off. I is wrong. Engagement partners should be rotated every seven years, not five years. Five years is the correct amount of time under PCAOB standards for a lead partner to be rotated off.

502. (C) A cash advance from a financial institution of $20,000 to be repaid within 10 days made under normal lending policies would impair independence. A, B, and D are wrong. Certain loans made under normal lending policies do NOT impair independence. Automobile loans, loans of the surrender value under the terms of an insurance policy, borrowings fully collateralized by cash deposits at the same financial institution, and credit cards and cash advances on checking accounts with a total unpaid balance of $10,000 or less do NOT impair independence if made under normal lending policies.